EDUCATIONAL EXPERIENCES OF HIDDEN HOMELESS TEENAGERS

Homeless youth face countless barriers limiting their ability to complete a high school diploma and transition to postsecondary education. Their experiences vary widely based on family, access to social services, and where they live. More than half of the 1.5 million homeless youth in America are in fact living "doubled-up," staying with family or friends because of economic hardship and often on the brink of full-on homelessness.

Educational Experiences of Hidden Homeless Teenagers investigates the effects of these living situations on educational participation and higher education access. First-hand data from interviews, observations, and document analysis shed light on the experience of four doubled-up adolescents and their families. The author demonstrates how complex these residential situations are, while also identifying aspects of living doubled-up that encourage educational success. The findings of this powerful book will give students, researchers, and policymakers an invaluable look at how this understudied segment of the adolescent population navigates their education.

Ronald E. Hallett is an Assistant Professor of Education at the University of the Pacific and a Research Associate in the Center for Higher Education Policy Analysis at the University of Southern California.

To the families who opened their homes to me.

EDUCATIONAL EXPERIENCES OF HIDDEN HOMELESS TEENAGERS

Living Doubled-Up

Ronald E. Hallett

Routledge
Taylor & Francis Group

NEW YORK AND LONDON

First published 2012
by Routledge
711 Third Avenue, New York, NY 10017

Simultaneously published in the UK
by Routledge
2 Park Square, Milton Park, Abingdon, Oxon OX14 4RN

Routledge is an imprint of the Taylor & Francis Group, an informa business

Library of Congress Cataloging in Publication Data
A catalog record has been requested for this book

ISBN13: 978-0-415-89372-5 (hbk)
ISBN13: 978-0-415-89373-2 (pbk)
ISBN13: 978-0-203-80600-5 (ebk)

Typeset in Bembo
by Taylor & Francis Books

Printed and bound in the United States of America on acid-free paper by Walsworth Publishing Company, Marceline, MO

CONTENTS

List of Tables and Figures   ix
Acknowledgements   x

1   Introduction   1

2   Resilience and Homeless Youth   9

3   Entering Their Lives and Homes   30

PART I
Separate Households   **41**

4   Isaac's Long Shot   43

5   Juan Dreams Big   56

PART II
Merged Residences   **69**

6   Kylee Goes with the Flow   71

7   Marco Plans to be Average   86

PART III
Analysis and Implications

PART III
Analysis and Implications   **101**

 8 Influence of Residential Structure   103

 9 Implications for Policy and Practice   123

10 Epilogue (18 Months Later)   130

Bibliography   133
Index   142

List of Tables and Figures

Tables

2.1 Models of Resiliency Theory 15

2.2 Risk and protective factors relevant to urban youth 22

3.1 Research sites—basic demographic information 33

3.2 Research participants—basic demographic information 34

8.1 Differing formations within doubled-up residences 109

8.2 Doubled-up youth and educational resilience 120

Figures

4.1 Isaac's house 44

5.1 Juan's apartment 57

6.1 Kylee's apartment 72

7.1 Marco's house 87

Acknowledgements

Many relationships formed, and a few dissolved, over the course of this project. I offer both appreciation and apology. Before beginning this process, I had the naïve assumption that a book was the sole accomplishment of an individual. Many people contributed to this book and deserve acknowledgement. I was fortunate to have an amazing group of mentors who supported and guided me through this daunting process. Pierrette Hondagneu-Sotelo provided consistent encouragement and advice. Amanda Datnow offered both high standards and praise throughout my development as a scholar. Kristin Ferguson met with me whenever I asked to discuss issues that framed this study. Bill Tierney expected perfection and provided the scaffolding to eventually come close to that standard.

I developed many personal and professional relationships with colleagues who enabled me to see this process through to the end. Zoe Blumberg Corwin, Margaret Sallee and Kristan Venegas served as my informal mentors by giving feedback on my writing and frequently allowing me to learn from their own experiences. Brianna Kennedy and Alejandra Velasco provided professional support and personal encouragement when I felt overwhelmed. In addition, Alex Masulis at Routledge patiently worked with me through the publishing process.

I was fortunate to have many individuals outside of the academic context who supported me. First and foremost, the youth and families whose stories are told in this book gave me access to their homes and allowed me the opportunity to share life with them. The relationship with my own parents also evolved over the course of this project into something more than I could have ever imaged. In addition, the congregation of a newly formed church in Long Beach, The Garden, pushed me to think beyond simply writing a book and move towards enjoying life with people. And Rock Harbor provided financial support that enabled me to provide many of the families with Christmas gifts. Finally, I want to thank Sarah Thomas-Sawin, a teacher from high school, who saw something more in me than the classes I skipped and the poor grades I earned. Although we have since lost touch, my hope is to eventually thank her for investing in me.

1

INTRODUCTION

"Tell me about where you live," I ask during our first interview.

"It's an apartment, we pay like about $880 dollars for rent, it is two bedrooms and I live with my mom, my brother, my sister, my grandparents, my aunt and my cousin," Juan explains. "My aunt and my cousin, they got their bedroom. My mom, my brother and sister got to share a bedroom, and there's a closet and they turned it into a bedroom for me. My grandparents is in the living room."

Juan shook my hand and sat in one of the maroon office chairs that surrounded the large table in the conference room near my office on campus. He wore tight black jeans with matching Vans and a baggy sweatshirt with his high school's name embroidered across the chest. Juan was the type of student that teachers love—a hardworking, compliant teenager who wanted to please. He finished the first semester of his senior year the week prior and eagerly looked forward to high school graduation. "I want to be a doctor," he smiled as he spoke about serving his community in the future. Although confident and outgoing around friends, Juan took a more submissive role with authority figures.

Juan lived in a modest two-bedroom apartment with seven other people at the time of our first meeting; however, his uncle would also move in a month later. Financial necessity forced his mother to choose between seeking welfare-based support through a homeless shelter and remaining in an apartment where she shared a bedroom with her three children. She refused to give up her independence by entering a shelter, and pride limited her willingness to rely on welfare programs. Juan's mother hoped to eventually secure an apartment independent of the other residents, but she barely scraped by each month. The family lived at the brink of economic disaster.

This residential situation falls into a subcategory of homelessness frequently overlooked—youth living doubled-up. The federal government has recognized the importance of supporting youth without residential stability, and legislation has been created that protects their access to public education. The *McKinney–Vento Homeless Assistance Act*, which frames how schools identify and serve homeless students, defines a homeless person as an individual lacking a fixed, regular and adequate night-time residence. The federal mandate specifically mentions youth who reside in shelters, welfare hotels, transitional programs or any place not ordinarily used as regular sleeping accommodations (e.g. streets, cars, movie theatres and abandoned buildings). McKinney–Vento also includes individuals who live doubled-up with another family due to economic crisis. The assumption is that families living doubled-up experience educational challenges similar to those living in other unstable environments and, therefore, require similar protections. The federal law primarily addresses issues of access for K–12 education. None of the provisions relates to higher education.

Homeless youth are not a homogenous group; their experiences differ depending upon their connection to parents, relationship with social service agencies and residential location (Tierney, Gupton & Hallett, 2008). For example, Juan's experiences living doubled-up differed from an adolescent living without parental guidance in an abandoned building or a family residing in a homeless shelter. Although youth living doubled-up represent more than half of the homeless youth population (National Center for Homeless Education, 2007), research focused on their residential experiences has been relatively thin. Little is known about how individuals and family units negotiate the tenuous relationships that form when forced to raise children without adequate space. Previous research has confirmed the magnitude of this issue, but less attention has been given to understanding how these families make choices about structuring the residence or how living doubled-up influences the educational participation of youth.

Distinguishing *homeless* from *housed* is complex. Poverty and housing exist on a continuum with many individuals and families transitioning between different forms of residential instability. The United States Department of Education expanded the definition of homelessness in accordance with McKinney–Vento to include "children and youths who are sharing the housing of other persons due to loss of housing, economic hardship, or a similar reason" (42 USC 11434a). The federal definition excludes families choosing to live together primarily for cultural reasons, as domestic partnerships, in roommate relationships or other situations unrelated to economic necessity. Differentiating between individuals choosing to live in a doubled-up residence and those forced to as a result of economic hardship is a complicated process. Individuals may, for example, choose to live with extended family members or friends in an effort to get additional support with childcare or to assist aging parents through their later years of life. Cultural custom may also require children live with parents until married. These "cultural choices" do not qualify under the federal definition of homeless. Although it is possible for a doubled-up residence to exist for cultural reasons, however, economic constraints can preclude the families from securing adequate space. Untangling the "choice" can be difficult, especially in low-income communities where economic necessity and cultural custom may overlap.

The youth presented in this book did not want to live in a doubled-up residence. Economic crises forced their parents to make this choice. This exploratory study furthers theoretical understanding of how youth without residential stability exhibit resilience. Since few studies have been conducted with doubled-up youth, I focus on understanding their experiences by entering their homes and providing a platform for them to share their voices. Limited space and economic crisis were common among the residences. My initial assumption that living doubled-up was a risk factor endured similarly by all youth proved to be misinformed. Structural differences framed the youth's experiences in distinct ways.

To understand why youth had different educational perceptions and outcomes, I focus on the risk and protective aspects of this residential arrangement that influenced participation in the educational process. The following questions frame the study: How do doubled-up youth define their social environments? How do the social environments influence educational perceptions and participation? How do the processes at work in the lives of doubled-up youth enhance or detract from their educational resilience? The following sections provide background on the issue of homelessness in urban areas with a focus on the relationship between residential instability and educational participation. I provide an overview of resilience, the theoretical framework guiding this study, before briefly introducing each of the participants and describing their residential context.

Purpose and significance of the study

Economic instability in the United States has created uncertainty for many Americans. Numerous families lost housing as a result of adjustable loans, and jobs have evaporated as the stock market dipped, banks filed for bankruptcy, and faith in government declined. The number of families living in doubled-up residences has steadily increased since 2006 (Erlenbusch *et al.*, 2008). Over 75% of those who have lost their homes to foreclosure sought refuge in the residences of their family or friends (Erlenbusch *et al.*, 2008). Parents in need of housing frequently turn to family and friends before seeking assistance in a homeless shelter. These parents must consider the impact moving may have on their children's educational progress. As a result, some families have chosen to "double-up" in order to remain in a desirable school district. Cuts in social service programs occurred in unison with the economic downslide. Families in lower income brackets share residences at higher rates than any other socioeconomic group. Although the national economic crisis increased the number of middle-class families living in shared residences, lower-income families were hit hardest by the economic downturn. Families living "paycheck to paycheck" without savings tend to be the first to lose housing when individual or societal economic crises occur. Lower-income families have shared residences for some time, but the recession forced many families to seek temporary refuge in the home of a friend or relative.

Youth and families living doubled-up frequently do not identify with the term *homeless*; however, personal identification with the word is not a requirement to fall under the protection of McKinney–Vento. In fact, many people protected by the law do not accept the term. The idea of "home" may differ dramatically from middle-class notions. Individuals living in shelters, cars, hotels or motels, and on the street may argue that they are not homeless because they have identified a space to reside and store their belongings (Wolch *et al.*, 2007). Marginalized populations often reject labels perceived to be derogatory or low status; however, social service programs require categorization (Mawhinney-Rhoads & Stahler, 2006; Toro & Warren, 1999). Laws, policies and procedures require definitional parameters in order to ensure finite resources are distributed to the intended recipients. The purpose of this book is not to argue that doubled-up youth are homeless—the goal is to understand how a group that has already been identified as homeless experiences the educational process. In addition to informing public policy and service imple- mentation, this study expands the current understanding of how networks influence educational persistence in low-income areas. Accordingly, the purpose is to understand how residential environments influence educational participation.

Completing a high school education is frequently a challenge, and at times irre- levant, to subpopulations of homeless youth because their focus is diverted to daily survival. Specifically, youth living on the street or in shelters have a difficult time navigating the educational process. Less is known about homeless families and youth living in precarious or semi-stable residences, for example, those living doubled-up. I build upon previous research that has found that homeless youth are not a homogenous group (Finley & Finley, 1999; Smith & Ferrari, 1997). They experience the educational process differently depending upon individual, family and community factors. Residential context influences how youth perceive education and resources available to support their participation in school. For example, youth living on the streets may be without adult supervision and involved in prostitution, substance use or illegal activities (Halcon & Lifson, 2004). The life experiences of these youth differ from those who live in a shelter as part of a family unit and follow strict rules to remain sheltered. Building upon the current understanding of the educational needs of homeless youth, I explore how youth living doubled-up are similar to and different from their homeless counterparts and low-income youth in general.

There are at least three reasons why a focus on doubled-up youth is warranted. First, doubled-up individuals are among the least studied of all subgroups of homeless youth; however, they compose the largest segment of individuals covered by McKinney–Vento. Between 3 and 4 million individuals experience homelessness each year in the United States, of which approximately 1.5 million are youth under 21 years of age (Fernandes, 2007; National Alliance to End Homelessness, 2006). Nearly 60% of youth identified as homeless by school sites nationwide live doubled-up as compared with 3% who are unsheltered, 7% living in hotels and 24% who live in shelters (National Center for Homeless Education, 2007). A growing body of research explores the experiences of specific subgroups of homeless youth (e.g. Freeman & Hamilton, 2008; Karabanow, 2008; Kidd, 2004; Witkin *et al.*, 2005). Understanding how these youth navigate and perceive the educational process can aid educators and policymakers in developing future programs and policy initiatives to support homeless youth. The federal government has determined that the educational needs of doubled-up youth are more similar to homeless youth than the general population. Implementation of the law has been problematic. Many school district employees report uncertainty, suspicion and conflict in identifying doubled-up families and determining how to distribute resources (Ascher & Phenix, 2006). In particular, administrators and enrollment managers suspect these families of abusing the law to acquire finite resources and sidestep rules about living within school boundaries. These concerns are magnified in overcrowded, under-resourced school systems. The result is resources intended to support educational participation may be withheld from doubled-up families and youth. This study offers an opportunity to explore the experiences of a frequently invisible subgroup. In particular, I focus on how the residential environment frames how youth participate in high school and transition to postsecondary education.

Second, living doubled-up is often a precursor to other forms of residential instability and part of a cycle of homelessness (O'Toole *et al.*, 2007). High housing costs coupled with limited affordable housing units has led to an increase in the number of families who live doubled-up (Dyrness, Spoto & Thompson, 2003). Families and individuals experiencing economic crises frequently seek the support of family or friends before contacting social welfare agencies (O'Toole *et al.*, 2007). Friends and relatives may be willing to share housing for a short period, but financial strain and overcrowded conditions limit the length of time a family is welcomed in another's home (Julianelle & Foscarinis, 2003). If network support runs out, the family has few other options than seeking refuge in a shelter, motel or vehicle (Rog & Buckner, 2007). Young adults from low-income families are particularly vulnerable to living in doubled-up arrangements because they leave home without fully developed social or economic resources (Wright *et al.*, 1998). Doubled-up residences are often the first step as individuals and families attempt to move out of homeless shelters. Tenuous and volatile economic situations make transition out of homelessness difficult. Therefore, families transitioning from a shelter to a doubled-up situation are also more likely to return to the street or a shelter than those who find independent housing (Wright *et al.*, 1998). Exploring risk and protective factors associated with this living arrangement may assist in developing programming and policies that can support families attempting to avoid moving into a homeless shelter.

Finally, the experiences of these youth allow for a critical discussion of the terms *home* and *homeless*. Owning a house is part of the American Dream. Middle-class notions of individualism often involve raising children in a single family dwelling. Living doubled-up goes against these perceptions of adequate space necessary for parenting. This residential arrangement is the gray area between being housed and homeless. Youth and families living doubled-up or homeless may experience shame as a result of an inability to meet this societal standard. Given that families living doubled-up live in an apartment or house, is it possible to have a home and still be homeless? Dissecting these underlying ideologies is an important component of reducing the amount of shame these families experience.

Organization of the book

In the chapters that follow, I discuss the experiences of four youth living in doubled-up residences. The lives and voices of these youth are used to understand the influence their residential situation had on their participation in high school. I focus on both risks associated with living in a doubled-up residence as well as protective factors that shaped how these youth perceived future opportunities. A note about terminology is warranted. The terms residence and household are frequently considered interchangeable. The complex nature of these environments warrants distinguishing between the two. I consider *residence* to encompass all individuals who live in a specified space (e.g. an apartment or house). I use *household* to refer to a family unit (e.g. a mother and her children). Therefore, a doubled-up residence is composed of several households.

Following this introductory chapter, I discuss two issues that frame this study: resilience and homelessness. Resilience explores how individuals succeed when faced with adversity. This framework allows for a strength-based approach to identifying risk and protective aspects of social environments. I focus on educational resilience, which concerns risk and protective factors associated with navigating the educational process. The uncertainty concerning residential stability negatively impacts how homeless youth engage in the educational process. As aforementioned, homeless youth are not a homogeneous group and their educational experiences differ. Youth living doubled-up have experiences that uniquely influence how they participate in the educational process. Since little is known about youth living doubled-up, I begin by exploring the risk and protective aspects of homeless youth in general with particular focus on those aspects influencing the educational process. Receiving a high school diploma and postsecondary degree has the potential of increasing access to jobs and careers that may afford these youth a more stable future.

Chapter 3 outlines the context of the study, including demographic information and an overview of the two areas of Los Angeles where the participants lived. I also discuss how I gained access to these residences and the relationships formed throughout the data collection process. Living doubled-up, and homelessness in general, frequently involves shame. Parents may fear social service agencies will remove their children; adolescents may fear social consequences if peers discover their residential arrangements. Understanding the context of the research process helps illuminate the complexity and instability of their residential environments. I needed to establish a trusting relationship with the family in order to gain access to their lives and homes.

The next two parts of the book demonstrate the complexity of the lives of these youth by providing a glimpse into their homes. The chapters in these parts begin with a description of each residential context as well as illustrating how space was allocated. The remainder of the chapter provides "a day in the life" of each teenager. Learning how these youth navigate life gives an outsider the opportunity to "see" how this often invisible population of students experiences life. I invite the reader to follow each youth through a day in their lives to get a sense of their individual personalities and residential contexts. Their experiences differed depending upon how families within the residence organized the home and delegated responsibilities. Two residential formations emerged: separate households and merged residences. Part I demonstrates how separate households attempted to function as individual units living alongside other families in the same space. The lack of collaboration led to conflict and negatively influenced the adolescents' educational participation. Part II focuses on how merged residences blended the multiple families into one unit. Division of labor limited the responsibility of each parent in the merged residence and allowed for more attention to be given to ensuring youth attended school.

The residential arrangements were not deterministic. Multiple facets of the youth's lives framed their educational participation. Chapter 8 explains how living doubled-up can serve both as a risk and protective factor. The educational resilience of the youth was framed by multiple factors, including school context and access to an educational mentor. The federal government has included doubled-up youth within the overall category of homeless youth because the assumption is that this residential formation involves instability and creates educational risks. I expected themes to emerge as I spent time with the participants that would explain the inherent risks of this residential formation. Specifically, I anticipated youth to have high rates of mobility, limited access to resources, and overcrowded residences that negatively influenced their participation in the educational process. If this held true, then living in a doubled-up residence would increase the risk of dropping out of high school. Since this hypothesis began with the assumption of inherent risk, resilient youth would have protective factors outside of the residence that led to successful adaptation. I found living doubled-up actually had the potential of both risk and protection. The interaction between the social network of the participants and their living environments worked together to frame how youth participated in the educational process. Recommendations based upon these findings are provided for practitioners, policymakers and researchers.

Introducing the youth

Before digging into theoretical arguments and previous research, an introduction to the youth is necessary to humanize the issue. Below is a brief summary of the youth and their residential situations. This serves as an introduction, but more importantly provides context for the discussion of doubled-up residences in the next two chapters.

Isaac was a 17-year-old with sophomore-level credits. A month before the study began he stopped attending an independent study school and did not actively participate in the educational process during the 2008–9 school year. He lived in a three-bedroom house and shared a room with his stepbrother and a 25-year-old roommate. His stepmother had her own room. The other bedroom was shared by his 15-year-old stepsister, 7-year-old stepbrother, and a 50-year-old roommate. His 20-year-old stepsister slept in the living room with her two young children.

Juan was a 17-year-old senior in high school. He was completing the requirements for a high school diploma and planned to attend the University of California in Los Angeles. He lived in a two-bedroom apartment. Juan shared a bedroom with his mother, 15-year-old brother, and 9-year-old-sister. His aunt and 14-year-old cousin lived in the other bedroom and his grandparents slept in the living room.

Kylee was a 16-year-old junior in high school who attended school on a daily basis and hoped to graduate in 2010. She failed a few classes during 9th and 10th grade, which she feared would delay graduation and limit postsecondary opportunities. She lived in a three-bedroom apartment. Her mother had one room and a female roommate had another room. Kylee shared a 10' by 12' bedroom with her 14-year-old sister, 12-year-old brother, and the roommate's two children who were in elementary school.

Marco was a 17-year-old senior in high school who was completing the requirements for a diploma and planned to enroll at California State University in Northridge. He lived in his aunt's four-bedroom house. He shared a bedroom with his father and 19-year-old sister. His aunt and uncle had one bedroom and each of the other rooms was occupied by an adult cousin.

2

RESILIENCE AND HOMELESS YOUTH

The federal government passed the *McKinney–Vento Homeless Assistance Act* to protect the educational rights of homeless youth. The mere existence of McKinney–Vento is a testament to the federal government's acknowledgement that homeless youth face unique educational challenges. McKinney–Vento requires states, districts and schools to review and modify any policies that create a barrier to homeless youth's participation in the educational process. This includes making available backpacks, uniforms and supplies free of charge as well as enrolling homeless youth immediately regardless of if transcripts and immunization records are available. These youth also get to stay at the same school when residential mobility occurs within district boundaries. Many of the mandates remain unfulfilled. For example, over 75% of school districts nationwide report that transportation barriers exist for homeless youth (National Center for Homeless Education, 2007). The law has undergone several revisions, including the controversial inclusion of doubled-up youth in the definition of homelessness.[1] State, local and district school staff have been slow to classify doubled-up youth under the protections of McKinney–Vento, in part due to suspicion that families may be abusing the law (Ascher & Phenix, 2006). None of the youth in this study was properly identified by the school district or took advantage of the legal protections. Kylee's mother was stunned to find out that a federal mandate existed that may offer assistance with enrollment, school supplies and uniforms.

McKinney–Vento focuses almost exclusively on increasing educational access. Although barriers exist, the majority of homeless youth express a desire to earn a high school degree and transition to college (Tierney, Gupton & Hallett, 2008). Kylee, for example, hoped to earn a college degree that would enable her to have a more secure and stable future. These aspirations may be difficult to achieve as many youth and families prioritize daily survival and immediate needs over the long-term goal of academic achievement (Stronge, 1993). Attending school regularly and persisting through graduation from high school is frequently a challenge for homeless students (Thompson, Zittel-Palamara & Maccio, 2004). Over 60% of homeless youth are not proficient in math or literacy (National Center for Homeless Education, 2007). The academic experiences during childhood often lead to low educational levels in adulthood. Nationally, nearly half of homeless adults are not high school graduates and fewer than 2% have a college degree (Bring Los Angeles Home, 2004; Thompson, Safyer & Pollio, 2001). A major barrier to college access for homeless youth is earning a high school diploma. Less than half of youth who become homeless earn a diploma or GED (Freeman & Hamilton, 2008).

Dismal educational outcomes of homeless youth have been explained by investigating environmental and network factors. Environmental risks involve factors in the community that influence how youth participate in the educational process. The lives of homeless youth are impacted by violence, including physical attack, sexual assault and observing violent acts (Kipke *et al.*, 1997b). The length of time spent unaccompanied on the street or in a shelter is linked with the probability of physical or sexual victimization (Greene, Ennett & Ringwalt, 1999). Exposure to violence, even when the individual is not personally involved, heightens the level of anxiety and fear experienced by the young person (Kipke *et al.*, 1997b). Homeless youth living in these communities are vulnerable to victimization and may become involved in deviant social networks that discourage educational participation (Greene, Ennett & Ringwalt, 1999; Tyler, Hoyt & Whitbeck, 2000). Homeless youth engage in high-risk behaviors more often than their housed peers, disrupting their educational participation. Specifically, homeless youth have increased rates of substance abuse, mental health disorders, sexual risk-taking and violence (Lifson & Halcon, 2001; Rew, Taylor-Seehafer & Fitzgerald, 2001; Thompson, Zittel-Palamara & Maccio, 2004). These youth experience high rates of depression and suicidal ideation (National Alliance to End Homelessness, 2006). Doubled-up individuals abuse substances less frequently than other subgroups of homeless persons, but significantly more often than the general population (Eyrich-Garg *et al.*, 2008). The environmental risks influence youth's attendance, focus and persistence in school.

Network risks concern the relationships youth draw upon to make choices. Homeless youth have networks that differ from their housed peers, including limited connection to school staff and difficulty forming long-term friendships (Greene, Ennett & Ringwalt, 1999; Kipke *et al.*, 1997b; Tyler, Hoyt & Whitbeck, 2000). These youth are highly mobile, moving between multiple residential and school locations (Decter, 2007). Mobility is associated with low rates of educational participation, and the impact on achievement increases as the individual gets older (Buckner, 2001). Higher rates of residential mobility negatively influence homeless youth's ability to form relationships with educational mentors and peers engaged in the educational process. The relationships doubled-up families form with friends and relatives enable them to avoid moving into a homeless shelter, hotel or car when economic crises initially occur (Bolland & McCallum, 2002). Karin Eyrich-Garg and colleagues (2008) found that doubled-up youth and families have stronger social support than other subgroups of homeless persons; however, stress placed on these relationships as a result of shared housing and limited resources often leads to a breakdown in the social network. After the social network is exhausted, the family enters a shelter or other forms of homelessness.

Although researchers have identified the participation rates and environmental risks that influence school attendance, two topics remain noticeably absent. First, researchers frequently approach the study of homeless youth from a deficit model by focusing on the risks that lead to negative outcomes (Edwards, Iritani & Hallfors, 2006; Rew, Taylor-Seehafer & Fitzgerald, 2001; Tyler, Hoyt & Whitbeck, 2000; Whitbeck & Simons, 1990). Such research typically highlights multiple risk factors and barriers that influence the choices homeless youth make; however, few studies explore the protective factors that enable some youth to successfully navigate the educational system. Second, the majority of these studies focus on homeless youth living in shelters and on the streets—two of the smallest subgroups of the homeless student population (e.g. Bassuk *et al.*, 1997; Lifson & Halcon, 2001; Rew, Taylor-Seehafer & Fitzgerald, 2001).

This study focuses on the largest subgroup of homeless youth and builds on previous work by using a strength-based approach to understand the experiences and resilience of youth living doubled-up. In order to understand the factors that frame how youth living doubled-up and homeless youth in general experience the educational process, I utilize resilience as a framework to identify the strengths of youth and their environment as well as risks. In particular, I focus on social network factors that influence educational resilience.

Educational resilience

Resilience is the successful adaptation of an individual despite risk and adversity (Fergus & Zimmerman, 2005; Masten, 1994) or unexpected achievement in spite of stress (Bartelt, 1994). Resilience is a term that is most meaningfully applied to persons who exhibit successful adaptation even though their environment or experiences place them at heightened risk for maladaptive outcomes (Buckner, Mezzacappa & Beardslee, 2003). The definition of resilience involves two components: successful adaptation and adversity (Masten & Coatsworth, 1998). Successful adaptation is frequently defined from an outcomes perspective (Zimmerman & Arunkumar, 1994). The researcher begins with outcomes that are expected of the general population (e.g. high school graduation or typical psychological development) and uses these outcomes as the measure of successful adaptation. Youth unable to reach these benchmarks or standards do not fall under the definition of resilience. Adversity is typically understood in terms of risk factors that may limit successful adaptation. Multiple studies have documented the correlation between risks (e.g. child abuse or poverty) and difficulty meeting developmental and educational benchmarks (Felner, 2005; MacLeod, 1987, 1995; Masten *et al.*, 1997; Willis, 1977). The researcher first identifies the adversity present and outlines what successful adaptation means before considering the resilience of an individual.

Scholars in the fields of psychology, sociology and anthropology have a long tradition of studying the experiences of low-income, urban youth. The challenges these youth face have been well documented, including gang violence, low-performing schools and high mobility rates (Kotlowitz, 1991; Kozol, 1995; LeBlanc, 2003; Stack, 1974). These findings have been useful for educators, policymakers and others interested in designing policies and creating programs to help youth overcome obstacles; however, the strength, persistence and community support present within these neighborhoods did not get the same level of attention. Resiliency Theory represents a shift in thinking—theorists attempt to understand how individuals succeed in the face of adversity. Resiliency theorists argue that some youth succeed in spite of risk factors or, more accurately, because of the presence of protective factors (Zimmerman & Arunkumar, 1994). Resilience from this perspective is defined in terms of psychological health, physical development and educational outcomes. Unlike studies focused on negative aspects of urban life, resiliency theorists use a strengths–based approach (Zimmerman & Arunkumar, 1994). The goal is to identify both the risks within a specific context as well as the protective processes. Initial studies examined the influence of risk factors in isolation; however, more recent research argues that accumulative risk better explains resilience (Masten & Powell, 2003). The achievement of resiliency theorists has been in realizing that "resilience in individual development had the potential to inform policy, prevention programs, and interventions" (Masten & Powell, 2003, p. 2).

Resiliency Theory evolved as a response to the deterministic tendencies of urban research. The focus moved from identifying conditions that resulted in specific outcomes to discussing the probability of success or failure (Rutter, 1985; Zimmerman & Arunkumar, 1994). This theoretical perspective supports the underlying assumption that risks present as a result of poverty during an individual's childhood may increase the likelihood of a similar lifestyle as an adult; however, resiliency theorists argue that these factors are better understood at the population level (Felner, 2005). The presence of risk does not determine outcomes for individuals. As the theory evolved, theorists have come to the conclusion that the presence of a single trait does not determine resiliency (Masten & Powell, 2003). Rather, a holistic view of the individual, family and community provides greater insight into the multitude of factors contributing the risk or protection.

Resiliency Theory has been used by several disciplines to understand behaviors ranging from substance abuse and teen pregnancy to persistence through post-secondary education (Durlak, 1998; McMillan & Reed, 1994; Shumow, Vandell & Posner, 1999; Waxman, Huang & Padron, 1997). In this study, I focus on the educational resilience of adolescents during the years youth are typically enrolled in high school. Scholars studying adolescents often use high school graduation as a benchmark of achievement and evaluate the students' engagement in academic activities or programs that assist youth through a degree or certificate completion (Gayles,

2005; Gonzalez & Padilla, 1997; Jackson & Martin, 1998; Randolph, Fraser & Orthner, 2004). Therefore, educational resilience involves reaching benchmarks in school when such an achievement is not expected due to risk.

The majority of researchers have focused on psychological or developmental resilience, but less attention has been given to educational resilience (Masten *et al.*, 1997). Jonathan Gayles (2005) defines educational resilience as "achievement when such achievement is rare for those facing similar circumstances or within a similar sociocultural context" (p. 250). Youth with academic resilience "sustain high levels of achievement motivation and performance despite the presence of stressful events and conditions that place them at risk of doing poorly in school and ultimately dropping out of school" (Alva, 1991, p. 19). Educational psychologists, in particular, define resilience in terms of "early traits, conditions, and experiences" (Wang, Haertel & Walberg, 1994, p. 46) or "a set of personality characteristics, dispositions, and beliefs" (McMillan & Reed, 1994, p. 139) that promote academic success regardless of the student's personal background. Studying motivation or belief systems enables educational psychologists to understand how perceptions influence participation.

I focus on actual participation in the educational process and the ability of individuals to complete postsecondary admission requirements. Using previous research as a basis, I define educational resilience as actively engaging in school and academic activities that enable an individual who may be at risk of dropping out to complete a high school diploma and transition to college. Two outcomes of interest from this perspective involve participation in the educational process and completion of transitional benchmarks including graduating from high school and transitioning to a postsecondary institution. Postsecondary preparedness refers both to understanding the process and taking steps towards admission in an institution of higher education. Therefore, a resilient high school student: 1) participates in the educational process; 2) meets the requirements necessary to graduate within the standard four-year period; and, 3) has taken steps necessary to transition to a college or university.

Focusing on educational issues with a resilience framework adds to the research on homeless youth in at least two ways. First, a study of doubled-up youth provides access to how this subgroup of homeless youth experiences residential instability. Second, using Resiliency Theory as a framework allows for a discussion of risks as well as identifying the protective aspects associated with this residential formation. This subgroup of students has low rates of school attendance and rarely transitions to postsecondary education. Studying how they experience both educational success and failure allows for a discussion of how to develop programs and policies that support them through the educational process.

Resilience research has its roots in, but differs from, risk research. Risk research seeks to identify aspects of the youth, family and community that correlate with undesirable outcomes (Luthar & Zelazo, 2003; Masten & Powell, 2003). The critique of risk research is that theories and findings focus on negative aspects of low-income, urban neighborhoods while overlooking positive attributes. These deficit-oriented views of low-income communities reinforce negative stereotypes by hyper-focusing on sensationalized risk factors and exploiting their experiences. Resiliency Theory evaluates risk; however, identifying protective qualities receives equal attention. Researchers identify individuals who have successfully reached predetermined benchmarks despite exposure to risks that correlate with failure. An individual who graduated from college after attending an under-resourced high school in a community where less than half of students complete high school would likely be identified as a resilient youth. The lives of these individuals can be studied in order to identify protective factors associated with positive outcomes. Reflecting on the factors present in the individual's life that assisted him or her through the educational process may lead to a better understanding of how to support other youth facing similar situations.

Considering the individual qualities of a youth's family dynamics and societal forces as both protective and limiting factors is a strength of Resiliency Theory. The study of risk and protective factors together allows for a more robust understanding of the processes influencing individuals being studied by identifying the presence of protective factors that override or neutralize risk factors (Dekovic, 1999). In place of approaches focused solely on barriers impeding success, identifying strengths provides information about what aspects of their life promote success. From a program development and public policy perspective, this approach enables researchers to make recommendations that build upon strengths of youth as well as addressing risks. Programs and policies can be created to facilitate access to these protective factors. Mentoring is but one example. Youth who have mentoring relationships focusing on navigating the educational process are more likely to transition to postsecondary institutions (Zimmerman & Bingenheimer, 2002). These findings can be used to develop college access programs for students attending low-performing schools.

Models of resilience

Over the past few decades four models of resilience have emerged: Invincibility, Challenge, Compensatory and Protective (see Table 2.1). The first two focus on how youth respond to risk factors whereas the Compensatory and Protective Models discuss the relationship between risk and protective factors. Each model is discussed below, including background information, how resilience is defined, and strengths and weaknesses.

Invincibility Model

The first model places youth into one of two categories: invincible or vulnerable. Both groups face similar risk factors; however, outcomes dramatically differ. Invincible or invulnerable youth are not influenced by obstacles and thrive beyond expectations, whereas vulnerable youth are unable to cope with the added stress. Invincibility assumes a level of innate predisposition to either success or failure. Scholars rarely ascribe to this model; however, the underlying assumptions have

TABLE 2.1   Models of Resiliency Theory

Model	View of resilience	Example
Invincibility	Invincible youth possess innate strength necessary to overcome obstacles that allow them to succeed when others fail	Two siblings experience the same risk factors. One drops out of school and the other graduates from college. Innate resilience determines outcomes
Challenge	Exposure to risk is a continuum. Low levels pose a short-term negative effect. Moderate exposure builds strength in the individual. High levels are insurmountable	A person exposed to poverty as a child may develop skills necessary to face hard economic times in the future. However, if poverty is severe and resources are too scarce during childhood, the person may develop a sense of hopelessness that negatively influences future decisions
Compensatory	The influence of protective and risk factors is added together to determine the influence on outcomes	An adolescent has high levels of stress as a result of family conflict. The influence of this stress is compared with self-esteem. Holding level of family conflict stable, the outcome will correlate with the level of the youth's self-esteem
Protective	Protective factors interact with risk factors. This interaction may reduce or remove the negative influence of risks	A young person without parental guidance may face a multitude of risks associated with school failure. A mentor can provide guidance necessary to counteract or defend against the impact of limited parental support

framed some popular texts and major motion pictures. For example, Ron Suskind (1999) portrays the plight of an urban youth from an inner-city high school to an elite private university, and Chris Gardner describes his journey from homelessness to the world of privilege (Gardner & Troupe, 2006). These individuals are assumed to have an innate level of inner strength that enables them to overcome obstacles, while their peers find similar situations insurmountable.

The majority of modern theorists challenge the assumption that individuals are born with a predisposition to either resilience or vulnerability (Glantz & Johnson, 1999; Johnson & Wiechelt, 2004). Those interested in developing programs and policies to support underserved youth find the invincibility perspective frustrating. If innate qualities determine outcomes then policies and programs are useless. Those with innate resilience will succeed; those with innate vulnerability will fail. Interventions would then be useless. Suniya Luthar and Dante Cicchetti (2000) argue that this perspective casts a negative shadow on individuals who do not succeed and does not fully capture resilience. Luthar and Cicchetti encourage researchers to consider the social processes that enable youth to develop resilience. They frame resilience as a process or phenomenon and remove the assumption that resilience is an innate quality or trait. Studies of identical twins raised in different households illustrate the importance of context on outcomes (Reiss *et al.*, 2000). Twins separated at birth have similar biological factors; however, outcomes may differ depending upon environmental conditions. Resilience is not a fixed attribute, but rather one influenced by the interaction between environmental and biological factors (Deater-Deckard, Ivy & Smith, 2005; Zimmerman & Arunkmar, 1994). The terms *invulnerability* and *invincibility* have largely been replaced by *resiliency* (Werner & Smith, 1992).

Challenge Model

The Challenge Model considers risk to be a continuum with a curvilinear view of resilience. The level of exposure frames how youth experience risk in an unexpected way. Risk can actually have protective qualities. Consider exposure to violence. Current findings indicate that "some exposure to risk, such as witnessing violence and family conflict, decreases adolescents' vulnerability to victimization, but at some point, the scales tip and too much risk increased the vulnerability to victimization" (Christiansen & Evans, 2005, p. 311). Minimal exposure to risk may result in a short-term negative outcome. The individual does not experience the risk for long enough or at a high enough level to develop a coping strategy. Witnessing one violent act may be traumatic without the person learning how to deal with similar situations in the future. Continued exposure at minimal or even moderate levels may strengthen the individual (Zimmerman & Arunkumar, 1994); however, enough of the risk factor must be experienced to elicit the development of a coping mechanism (Fergus & Zimmerman, 2005). These individuals develop skills and protective devices to manage the specific risk, which prepares them to deal with similar situations in the future. Living in a neighborhood where the potential of violence exists may allow a person to develop strategies to protect himself or herself as well as developing coping mechanisms that limit psychological distress if a similar act occurs in the future. Risk can become protective if a coping strategy develops that proves useful in the future when similar events occur. At some point the risk becomes insurmountable and experiences negatively influence the individual's ability to deal with future events. Constant exposure to violence may make a person feel helpless. This model views resilience as the ability to develop coping mechanisms through moderate exposure to risk without becoming overwhelmed.

The Challenge Model illustrates the complex nature of urban life. Exposure to risk may have both positive and negative influences. The underlying assumption aligns with development theories that suggest experiences during early development influence later behaviors and perceptions. In this case, lack of exposure or over-exposure may limit a person's ability to navigate future challenges. Resilience, from this perspective, becomes part of the developmental process, in which youth mobilize resources and learn from previous experiences (Yates, Egeland & Sroufe, 2003).

Although the Challenge Model has been conceptually useful in exploring how risk may be experienced, it has been difficult to test or use by practitioners. The point at which a factor shifts from protective to risk has been difficult to determine and may differ for each individual. The theory has limited utility for policymakers and practitioners unless the point at which exposure becomes a burden can be identified. In addition, the model considers each risk factor individually. As aforementioned, the majority of scholars argue that accumulated risk from multiple factors better explains the experiences of urban youth. Finally, this model does not consider the influence of protective factors that may alleviate risk. The following two models address these concerns.

Compensatory Model

The Compensatory Model acknowledges the impact of risk factors, but argues that protective factors can offset negative outcomes. This model considers the ability of certain protective factors to counteract or neutralize exposure to risk (Zimmerman & Bingenheimer, 2002). Risk factors are not removed from the person's life as a result of the protective factor—only the outcome changes. This is an additive model that quantifies the influence of protective and risk factors. High levels of protection as compared with risk lead to positive outcomes. Conversely, high levels of risk as compared with protection lead to negative outcomes. An adolescent may experience stress as a result of family conflict. The level of stress is compared with the student's self-esteem. Holding family conflict stable, outcomes will correlate with the level of each individual's self-esteem. This model of resilience generally explains resilience as the mediation of negative outcomes through the presence of protective factors (Johnson & Wiechelt, 2004). Researchers using this model attempt to identify risk factors connected to specific benchmarks (e.g. high school graduation or psychological health). After risk factors are identified, the goal is to find protective factors that compensate for the negative influence.

The previous models assume that youth face risk factors in a vacuum, but the Compensatory Model views resilience as a dynamic process involving interactions between the individual and environment (Johnson & Wiechelt, 2004; Zimmerman & Arunkumar, 1994). This approach enables recommendations to be made concerning the creation of public policies and programs that support the inclusion of protective factors to compensate for risks.

This model has at least two limitations. First, it does not account for the individual's ability to learn from the presence of risk—as the Challenge Model supports. Second, the model does not address interactions between protective and risk factors; rather, the two processes are held in isolation and only outcomes change. The

Protective Model, discussed in the next section, argues that protective factors can interact with risk and allow youth to avoid negative outcomes.

Protective Model

The Protective Model is the most frequently studied. This model argues that protective factors have the ability to shield an individual from a negative outcome or, in some cases, eliminate the risk altogether (Zimmerman & Arunkumar, 1994). A protective factor interacting with risk before an outcome occurs may have a moderating effect that leads to a positive outcome (Cowen & Work, 1988; Werner & Smith, 1982). To illustrate this point, consider a high school student who attends a low-performing school that has a culture of low aspirations and few students who intend to transition to postsecondary education. A college mentor can offset the negative environmental influences by giving the youth access to information about the educational process and offering encouragement. The student may not only be protected from the negative outcome, but also from engaging in behaviors that may result in additional risk.

Theorists using the Protective Model generally agree that interaction between risk and protection influences outcomes; however, two explanations exist concerning how this occurs. The Protective-Stabilizing approach suggests that the presence of a protective factor results in a stable outcome as the level of risk increases. The Protective-Reactive approach suggests that the presence of protective factors decreases, but does not completely remove, the influence on outcomes. Discussing this in the context of an adolescent raised in an urban neighborhood plagued by violence may help distinguish between the two approaches. From the Protective-Stabilizing perspective, a mentor may neutralize the influence of gang violence for all students whether or not they have direct connections with the gang (e.g. a sibling who is a member). The protective factor yields similar outcomes for all youth exposed to a specific risk. The Protective-Reactive perspective suggests that a mentor may have a positive influence, but outcomes will vary as exposure or connection to gang violence increases.

The Protective Model has been the most widely accepted for two reasons. First, connections between risk and protective factors have been easier to identify than connecting outcomes to innate qualities or determining at what point factors shift from protective to risk. Second, the Protective Model is useful for public policy and program development. If a connection can be drawn between a specific protective factor and the mitigation of risk, then programs and policies may be developed to provide youth access to the protective factor. Similar to the Compensatory Model, this perspective does not explain or allow an individual to develop protective skills as a result of exposure to risk. A binary is assumed. Risk factors lead to negative consequences and protective lead to positive.

The models discussed above involve risk and protective factors. The next section provides a discussion of specific categories of risk and protection. In particular, I focus on those related to educational participation of youth in urban areas.

Risk and protective factors

A clear understanding of the term *factor* is warranted. Early research looked for specific traits of the individual or environment that related to outcomes. The quantitative designs, typically collecting point-in-time data, viewed factors as fixed. More recently, researchers have begun to recognize that youth and environments are not static; rather, the presence of a variable, its influence and the individual's response may change over time (Deater-Deckard, Ivy & Smith, 2005). The varied response may be a result of learning a coping strategy, such as outlined in the Challenge Model, or related to the individual's development. As a child increases in age, he or she will have more life experiences to draw upon as well as increased cognitive abilities. Mastering language enables a more clear expression of how he or she feels and physical maturity may allow removal of self from environments of high risk. I use the term factor to identify complex processes that relate to outcomes; I do not assume that the youth's environment or response to factors will remain the same.

Up to this point I have discussed risk and protective factors as separate groups, which is both accurate and deceptive. Risk and protection often involve the same general categories (e.g. social network and personal attributes); however, characteristics of the factor and how the individual experiences it determine categorization. Family contexts may involve both protection (e.g. encouragement and access to resources) and risk (e.g. abuse and heath concerns), at times simultaneously within the same household.

In the sections that follow, I provide a more thorough definition of risk and protection. I place these terms within the context of poverty, which frames this study and has been one of the major foci of resilience research. I then discuss two general categories of factors: personal attributes and social networks. It is important to note that youth in low-income, urban neighborhoods are not at "high risk." They live in environments where many risk factors may be present, but each person living in urban areas should not be considered a high risk for failure (Felner, 2005; Felner *et al.*, 2000).

Definitions and background

Research on risk has a longer history than protection. The phrase *risk factor* comes from medical studies designed to identify aspects of biology, family history and lifestyle common to individuals diagnosed with heart disease (Costello & Angold, 2000). The goal was to identify factors predictive of heart disease and, subsequently, create prevention programs to limit future diagnoses. Several factors correlated with heart disease at the population level, including hypertension, obesity, lack of exercise and smoking; however, no single factor was common to all patients diagnosed (Sameroff, Gutman & Peck, 2003). A different combination of factors was necessary to explain each individual's diagnosis. These findings led to a discussion of risks that could be avoided to limit the likelihood of developing heart disease.

Social scientists and educational psychologists draw from this framework to identify risks that lead to a range of outcomes. Risk factors are broadly considered "those conditions that are associated with higher likelihood of a negative outcome" (Dekovic, 1999, p. 669). These aspects of the youth or environment increase the probability of a negative result, but do not predict outcomes (Durlak, 1998). Exposure to one or many of these factors did not guarantee failure, but a negative correlation increased in magnitude as risks accumulated in number and over time (Johnson & Wiechelt, 2004; Middlemiss, 2005). Isolated risk factors rarely correlated with outcomes at the population level, leading to a shift in considering the cumulative risk of complex psychological and social issues (Durlak, 1998; Johnson & Wiechelt, 2004; Sandler, 2001).

Several risk factors have been identified that influence educational participation of youth living in low-income communities. Family dynamics may increase risk of school failure, including family instability, single parenthood, chronic or severe poverty, and abusive households (Fergus & Zimmerman, 2005). Frequent mobility and attending multiple schools also increase the risk of academic difficulties (Corwin, 2008). Exposure to one or many of these factors does not guarantee that a student will fail, but a negative correlation increases in magnitude as risks accumulate in number and over time (Johnson & Wiechelt, 2004).

One overarching risk—poverty—frames the majority of research done with urban youth. Over 40 years ago, Herbert Birch and Joan Gussow (1970) connected poverty with multiple factors that lead to low education levels and difficulty securing employment. Birch and Gussow argued that the relationship between poverty and employment led to failures over the individual's life span and resulted in a cycle of poverty passed on to children. The connection between poverty and employment, which was the basic assumption of Birch and Gussow's theory, continues to influence modern theories; however, the deterministic premise has been challenged. They argued that low income levels limit parental access to resources and employment, which creates a cycle difficult to escape. More recently, the correlation between poverty and outcomes is discussed without assuming a deterministic cycle exists (Garmezy, 1991). Income levels no longer serve as the only marker of poverty, because families with the same income can have dramatically different neighborhoods and living arrangements (Felner, 2005). Social network and community factors are considered in conjunction with income.

Protective aspects of urban families and communities have been studied far less than risk factors (Christiansen & Evans, 2005; Dekovic, 1999; Kazdin, 1993). Protective factors are events, personality traits or relationships that alleviate the negative influence of risk factors (Durlak, 1998). These personal, social and institutional resources foster competence and promote successful development, which decrease the likelihood of engaging in problem behaviors (Dekovic, 1999). Youth who attend schools with teachers and counselors who offer support navigating the educational process may be more engaged in school and less likely to participate in risky behaviors (Dekovic, 1999; Masten et al., 1988; Willis, Vaccaro & McNamara, 1992). An assumption exists that in urban neighborhoods individuals cannot rely on either peers or parents. Both can be essential parts of a student's network by providing encouragement and support through the process of completing high school and transitioning to college (Tierney & Colyar, 2009). The racial, socioeconomic and linguistic composition of a youth's family and community may differ from a middle-class, White neighborhood—that does not mean they lack vital educational supports. Income may be lower, but a wealth of support may be available that encourages a student to participate in the educational process and pursue postsecondary aspirations (Yossi, 2005). Access to a protective factor does not guarantee academic success; however, a strong positive correlation exists. Resiliency Theory is less deterministic than theoretical perspectives that attempt to identify specific conditions that lead to an outcome (Rutter, 1985). The lives and development of adolescents in urban settings is complex; suggesting one factor could predict either success or failure is shortsighted. Resiliency perspectives allow for discussions of the probability of success or failure in a more complex and comprehensive way.

Two general categories of factors have been identified: personal attributes and social network factors (Garmezy, 1985; Masten & Powell, 2003). Table 2.2 provides an overview of each category. The following sections discuss aspects of each that may lead to risk or protection.

Personal attributes

Research on personal attributes generally comes from the fields of medicine and psychology. Overall health, physical disabilities, cognitive development, personality and other factors are studied to understand their relationship to medical or psychological disorders (Fergusson & Horwood, 2003; Rutter, 2001; Vance, 2001). As with any study, the researcher makes decisions about the focus. I provide a brief overview of personal attributes that correlate with educational participation, but I give less attention to the psychological and medical factors since this study is designed to explore the relationship between residential stability and educational participation.

Personality traits, good intellectual functioning and other personal attributes may influence how a youth approaches risk factors (Buckner, Mezzacappa & Beardslee, 2003; McMillan & Reed, 1994). For example, an individual with a positive attitude may be more likely to persist when a task is difficult and teachers may be more inclined to support the student through the process as compared with a student with a negative attitude. Positive attributes associated with mental and physical health generally increase self-concept and the belief that risk factors can be endured (Rausch, Lovett & Walker, 2003).

Developing coping skills enables youth to persist when faced with challenging neighborhoods, low-performing schools and complex family environments (Fergus & Zimmerman, 2005). Resilient youth develop emotional regulation (Cicchetti, Ackerman & Izard, 1995; Cicchetti & Lynch, 1993) and good problem-solving skills

TABLE 2.2   Risk and protective factors relevant to urban youth

Factor	Example of risk created	Example of protective quality
Mental health	Youth with psychological issues may be unable to participate in a typical school environment, which limits access to peers and mentors engaged in the educational process	A good temperament and appealing personality allow youth to deal with risk factors and enable them to build a positive social network
Physical health	Physical health concerns may similarly lead to frequent absences from school as a result of medical appointments or inability to participate in specific activities	Physical health and cognitive abilities enable youth to fully participate in the educational process, friendships and extracurricular activities
Neighborhood and peers	Isolated neighborhoods with minimal resources may limit access to middle-class peers and result in low aspirations	Neighborhoods with safe environments and natural mentors provide youth the support necessary to participate in school. Positive peer models provide youth an example to emulate
Family	Physical abuse or parental neglect is related to health problems and social development, which can influence educational participation	Stable family structures and encouragement from a parent or guardian help youth persist and develop educational aspirations
School	Frequently transitioning between schools disrupts relationships formed with peers, teachers and other educational mentors. Youth in low-performing schools have lower levels of achievement and drop out of school more frequently	Success in school and participation in extracurricular activities create a sense of accomplishment. These environments connect youth with adult role models that may offer encouragement and guidance

(Anthony, 1987; Murphy & Moriarty, 1976). These biological qualities frame how individuals interact with their environment. Youth who perceive competence in one aspect of their life (e.g. sports or academics) are more likely to avoid mental illness and develop persistence necessary to complete school (Seifer *et al.*, 1992; Werner & Smith, 1992). However, the youth needs to establish realistic expectations. If goals and aspirations are set beyond what the youth is capable of achieving, he or she may become discouraged when failure results (Werner & Smith, 1982; Wyman et al., 1991). Participating on the high school basketball team may help a student build social connections and develop confidence in self that could encourage persistence through difficult academic courses, but discouragement may result if an average athlete assumes an athletic scholarship will be his or her pathway to college. Although an innate predisposition may increase the likelihood of developing mental illness, aspects of the youth's environment and social network influence his or her development.

As aforementioned, resilience research began by focusing on innate qualities that influenced resilience. Biological factors contribute to resilience, but youth are not born resilient or vulnerable. Rather, specific biological factors may contribute to either risk or protection. Cognitive ability and genetic predisposition to disease relate to a student's ability to participate in the educational process (Johnson & Wiechelt, 2004; Kaplan, 2005). Youth may be born with dispositions or health issues that predispose them to specific outcomes; however, the environment shapes how personal attributes develop.

Social networks

An individual's social network influences access to both protective and risk factors. Youth are more likely to be resilient if they have stable social networks with few interruptions caused by conflict or geographic mobility (Jackson & Martin, 1998). Youth in poverty rarely have access to adults and peers with information about how to successfully navigate the educational process (Stanton-Salazar, 1997, 2001). As a result, many low-income youth develop low aspirations based upon perceived limited future opportunities (MacLeod, 1987, 1995; Willis, 1977). Youth anticipating future unemployment or a working-class job may disengage from school because they do not perceive the future relevance of attending class or completing assignments (Eckert, 1989; Willis, 1977). Nevertheless, the size and depth of social networks are not deterministic; youth in low-income areas may desire to achieve and take steps towards their goals in spite of barriers (Fordham, 1996; Stanton-Salazar, 1997, 2001; Willis, 1977). Three aspects of social networks are of particular importance to educational resilience: family, neighborhood and school.

Family

Family characteristics shape how a child prepares for and understands the educational process (Adams & Christenson, 2000; Walberg, 1984). Family dynamics may increase risk, including family instability, single parenthood, chronic or severe poverty, and abusive households (Fergus & Zimmerman, 2005; Ferguson, 2009; Johnson & Wiechelt, 2004; Sheridan, Eagle & Dowd, 2005). Individuals living in low-income communities often have complex family relationships that impact on how they approach and understand future relationships, employment and education (LeBlanc, 2003). Parents can positively influence resilience by nurturing a close bond with children, monitoring peer relationships, and protecting their children from high-risk environments (Cauce *et al.*, 2003). This type of parenting may be difficult for urban parents living in neighborhoods with multiple risks where survival consumes their time (Cauce *et al.*, 1996). The external problems youth exhibit in school may be explained by dysfunctional family relationships (Dekovic, 1999). For example, parents with physical or mental health concerns may have limited time and energy to monitor activities and cultivate a nurturing relationship with their children (Jackson & Martin, 1998). Family conflict may disrupt relationships and break bonds that support resilience (Christiansen & Evans, 2005). Conflict between parents may culminate in separation and a single parent, most often the mother, takes responsibility for raising the children (Jackson & Martin, 1998).

Family structure and parental participation in the educational process can be protective factors. Resilient youth generally have the opportunity to establish a close bond with at least one parent or caregiver who provides needed attention and support (McMillan & Reed, 1994). A two-parent family is desirable (Rausch, Lovett & Walker, 2003); however, the number of parents is less important than the parenting style (McMillan & Reed, 1994). A good parent–child relationship with supportive attachments serves as a protective factor. Youth have better outcomes if their parents monitor behavior and social relationships (Buckner, Mezzacappa & Beardslee, 2003; Christiansen & Evans, 2005). Resilient youth generally have a parent or caregiver who values education and views school as the route to a stable life (Jackson & Martin, 1998). In one study, youth who displayed resilience had parents who were involved in the students' education and 70% participated in the Parent–Teacher Association (Rausch, Lovett & Walker, 2003). Also, a positive correlation exists between the parents' level of education and their children's resilience (McMillan & Reed, 1994).

Youth do not always have access to parents. An unaccompanied homeless youth lives without a parent or adult caregiver. Some of these youth have fled abusive homes or left foster care placement. Resilient youth find substitute caregivers to compensate for limited family support (Corwin, 2008). These students build relationships with at least one adult in their personal life (guardian, mentor or member of extended family) and someone from school (teacher, counselor or coach). These trusting relationships provide encouragement and support necessary to navigate the educational process without parental support (McMillan & Reed, 1994).

Neighborhood

Low-income areas are frequently isolated from middle- and upper-class neighborhoods, a problem exacerbated by voluntary housing segregation of middle- and upper-class parents (Holme, 2002). Urban schools in these areas often end up segregated by race and socioeconomic status. The youth in these communities frequently have fewer relationships with individuals and agencies that facilitate access to information about resources and opportunities offered their middle-class peers (Tierney & Hallett, forthcoming). Instead, low-income communities tend to interact with government agencies, such as welfare, juvenile justice and foster care, more regularly than their peers in middle-class neighborhoods. An overdependence on social service agencies can create generational poverty associated with crime and incarceration. Michael Lipsky (1980) argues that street-level bureaucrats (i.e. social workers, police and court officials) interact with individuals in need of support and determine how perceived finite resources will be distributed. The system inadvertently distributes the minimal amount of resources needed for survival, but not enough for individuals and families to rise out of poverty. People being served are rarely voluntary participants in this process.

Neighborhoods provide the context for where childrearing and learning occur. Violence, social welfare agencies and mentors are a few aspects of the neighborhood that influence educational participation. Between 2002 and 2006, nearly 900,000 children each year in the United States were victims of maltreatment, including neglect and physical, sexual or psychological abuse (US Department of Health and Human Sciences, 2006). The rate of assault among adolescents has increased sevenfold since the 1950s (Garbarino, 2001). Youth exposed to physical and sexual violence are at risk for a range of adverse outcomes, including conduct problems, anxiety and depression, cognitive dysfunction, poor school performance, low-self esteem, and difficulties with peers (Margolin & Gordis, 2000). Living in an unstable or dangerous environment may encourage urban youth to use violent activity as a coping mechanism (Garbarino, 2001). A traumatic event, such as a murder or loss of housing, can create psychological instability; some youth express their inner turmoil outwardly through reckless behavior or violent acts (Rosenfeld, Lahad & Cohen, 2001). Problem behaviors, including depression and antisocial behavior, are more prevalent among youth exposed to violence (Jaffee, 2005). Youth who engage in substance abuse, violent behavior or sexual risk-taking experience increased rates of school failure (Fergus & Zimmerman, 2005).

Youth with violence in their lives are less resilient (Cauce et al., 2003). Even if the young person is not the primary victim, being a witness to violent acts increases the risk of developing psychological disorders (Christiansen & Evans, 2005). The lives of homeless youth are impacted by violence, including physical attack, sexual assault and observing violent acts (Kipke et al., 1997a). The length of time spent unaccompanied on the street or in a shelter is linked with the probability of physical or sexual victimization (Greene, Ennett & Ringwalt, 1999). Exposure to violence heightens the level of anxiety and fear (Kipke et al., 1997b).

Neighborhoods with limited violence and a sense of cohesion provide space for youth to develop resilience (Christiansen & Evans, 2005). The neighborhood influences peer relationships and opportunities for mentoring. Peers play an important role, both as a risk and protective factor (Dekovic, 1999). Youth with peers who model academic success are more likely to engage in the educational process and graduate. For example, youth in foster care benefit from friends in stable living environments who are experiencing academic success (Jackson & Martin, 1998). Youth may receive emotional reassurance as well as academic support and advice from peer interactions (Berndt, 1990). These relationships have the potential to mitigate the negative effects of adverse family circumstances and limit the impact of negative peer pressure (Jessor, 1991; Quinton et al., 1993).

The community influences access to natural mentors—individuals within the youth's family or social network who provide guidance. Geographic location frames who an individual interacts with on a regular basis. Natural mentoring relationships outside of the family can develop with teachers, neighbors or members of the youth's church and may influence attitudes towards school, drug use, violence and academic performance (Rausch, Lovett & Walker, 2003; Zimmerman & Bingenheimer, 2002). Meeting with a significant adult who offers consistent support and encouragement can have positive impacts on the youth's development and educational participation (Jackson & Martin, 1998). Mentoring programs have been established in communities to provide additional opportunities for these relationships to form.

School

Over 20% of students in the United States live below the poverty threshold (Planty et al., 2008). These students drop out of high school at six times the rate of their higher-income peers (Wirt et al., 2004). Families living in poverty typically live in poor communities and their children attend schools with a student body primarily composed of other low-income students (Kozol, 2005). These youth face many challenges to completing a high school degree and transitioning to postsecondary education, including lack of academic preparation and access to information. Racial disparities continue to exist—African Americans and Hispanics are more likely than White youth to live below the poverty line (Dounay, 2006; Planty et al., 2008; Zarate & Pachon, 2006).

Low-income students generally are less academically prepared during high school (Perna, 2006; Perna & Swail, 2001). Disparity between the structure and resources of high schools in low-income communities and more privileged communities plays a role in academic preparation. Access to high school Advanced Placement courses is but one example. High schools in low-income communities offer fewer Advanced Placement courses and less variety in course offerings (Dougherty, Millor & Jian, 2006; Klopfenstein, 2004). Students in these schools are less likely to pass the end-of-course exam, which correlates with college acceptance, access to elite post-secondary institutions and postsecondary course credit (Dounay, 2006; Zarate & Pachon, 2006). Youth enrolled in these classes report that teachers assigned to the class lack adequate training, school structure limits access to classes, and the student selection process negatively influences quality of classes (Hallett & Venegas, 2011). Adelman (2006) argues that academic rigor and quality high school curriculum correlate with postsecondary success; however, many youth in low-income communities lack access to either quality or rigor.

Lack of access to academic information reduces educational opportunities for youth in low-income communities. Unfortunately, students from low-income, minority schools have unequal access to the vital community networks that provide informal information about academic success (Yonezawa, Wells & Serna, 2002). For example, schools in poor communities have high student-to-counselor ratios that limit the amount of individualized attention students receive (Corwin *et al.*, 2004; McDonough & Calderone, 2006). Frequent mobility and attending multiple schools increase the risk of academic difficulties (Rausch, Lovett & Walker, 2003). Students face different teaching methods and curriculum at each school they attend; tracking mobile students and record keeping becomes a challenge for schools (Epstein, 1996). These aspects of the educational process increase the likelihood of repeating at least one grade level. Being retained, even in elementary school, is connected to lower high school graduation rates (Randolph, Fraser & Orthner, 2004).

Several studies have found a connection between school engagement and decreased risk (Dekovic, 1999). Learning to read fluently at an early age increases the likelihood of participating in the educational process (Jackson & Martin, 1998). Involvement in school activities and other organizations helps students learn how to manage time, navigate social relationships and take on leadership positions (McMillan & Reed, 1994). These opportunities frequently lead to relationships with peers and adults who are engaged in the educational process and can increase a student's access to academic resources (McNeal, 1995). Involvement in extracurricular activities has the potential of compensating for risk factors correlated with low levels of academic participation (Randolph, Fraser & Orthner, 2004).

Homeless youth and resilience

Few studies have used Resiliency Theory to understand the experiences of homeless youth. Research with these youth has primarily focused on identifying risks associated with residential instability, but little attention has been given to protective factors that may be present. Risks associated with homelessness include mental health concerns, increased sexual activity, and substance use.

Mental health scholars have found that homeless youth exhibit high rates of hopelessness and depression that influence how they approach services (Rew, Taylor-Seehafer & Fitzgerald, 2001; Unger *et al.*, 1998). Even among very poor families, homelessness appears to be associated with fewer resources and more adversity (Masten *et al.*, 1993). Homeless youth are exposed to violence at higher rates than those housed and experience behavior problems, social isolation and rejection, and conflict with parents (Anooshian, 2005). The psychological impact of residential instability and the increased exposure to risk factors influence how youth prepare for and engage in the educational process.

Homeless youth report more mental and physical health problems than their housed peers. Youth, specifically those unaccompanied, experience high rates of depression (Kurtz, Jarvis & Kurtz, 1991; National Alliance to End Homelessness,

2006; Thompson, Zittel-Palamara & Maccio, 2004; Yates *et al.*, 1988). Thompson, Zittel-Palamara and Maccio (2004) spent a year interviewing youth within 48 hours of registering at a youth shelter in New York. Nearly 75% of youth reported suffering from depression and contemplating suicide. Suicidal ideation and suicide attempts are significantly higher for homeless youth than their housed peers (Rew, Taylor-Seehafer & Fitzgerald, 2001; Thompson, Maguin & Pollio, 2003; Yates *et al.*, 1988). Sean Kidd (2004) found that attempting suicide was associated with feeling worthless, lonely, hopeless and trapped. Youth associated these emotions with the fear of being homeless indefinitely. Unaccompanied females living on the street are more likely than males to suffer from mental health issues (Whitbeck, Hoyt & Yoder, 1999). A sense of helplessness to remove this social stigma leads some youth to contemplate and attempt suicide (Kidd, 2004; Rew, Taylor-Seehafer & Fitzgerald, 2001).

Homeless youth often have home environments that are characterized by limited parental structure, physical or mental abandonment by parental figures, and substance abuse among caregivers (Ferguson, 2009). Unaccompanied homeless youth engage in risky sexual behavior at higher rates than their housed counterparts (Halcon & Lifson, 2004; MacKellar *et al.*, 2000). One study found that 70% of youth living on the street between the ages of 13 and 20 had engaged in unprotected sex with at least one partner over the past six months (MacKellar *et al.*, 2000). Their sexual patterns often lead to increased rates of pregnancy (Greene & Ringwalt, 1998) and sexually transmitted diseases (Rew, Fouladi & Yockey, 2002). Exposure to violence and engaging in sexual activity relate to substance abuse. Homeless youth, specifically those living on the street or in shelters, consume alcohol, smoke cigarettes or use illegal drugs at higher rates than their housed counterparts (Ensign & Santelli, 1998; Lifson & Halcon, 2001; Rew, Taylor-Seehafer & Fitzgerald, 2001; Thompson, Zittel-Palamara & Maccio, 2004). Lynn Rew and colleagues (2001) studied youth in Texas and found that more than 60% of youth started using alcohol and drugs before the age of 12. As substance abuse increases, youth are more likely to engage in "survival sex" to gain access to food, shelter and money (Greene, Ennett & Ringwalt, 1999). Homeless youth engage in survival sex at a significantly higher rate than their housed peers (Edwards, Iritani & Hallfors, 2006; Greene, Ennett & Ringwalt, 1999).

Homeless youth share many characteristics with their low-income peers, but aspects of their residential context differentiate how they experience the educational process. Several studies comparing homeless and low-income youth have found that homelessness poses additional educational challenges, including high rates of mobility and limited access to resources (e.g. Culhane *et al.*, 2003; Ensign & Santelli, 1998; Shinn *et al.*, 1998). High rates of mobility disrupt social connections and engagement in the educational process (Ferguson *et al.*, 2010). Being homeless or running away as a youth is positively correlated with adult homelessness (Simons & Whitbeck, 1991). Several vulnerable groups are overrepresented, including African American and Latino youth (Thompson, Zittel-Palamara & Maccio, 2004), foster youth who have emancipated or run away from placement (National Alliance to

End Homelessness, 2006), and gay, lesbian, bisexual and transgendered youth (Freeman & Hamilton, 2008).

Although studies have identified multiple risks associated with homelessness, little is known about aspects of these youth's environment that enable some youth to develop resilience. Bender and colleagues (2007) found that street youth may develop an ability to locate resources, solve daily problems, develop interpersonal skills, and establish a peer network. Those who developed these skills were able to meet daily needs and build a sense of community with others on the street. Mitchell Duneier (1999) studied street vendors in New York, the majority of whom were men living on the street or in semi-stable environments. Duneier found that street vendors developed and nurtured close relationships with each other. Their livelihood required social interactions with each other and the housed public. As a result, a system of rules was established. Elliot Liebow (1993) studied homeless women living in a shelter. Similar to Duneier, he found that the women in his study developed friendships and relied on each other for emotional support. Many of these women could identify a specific incident or series of events that led to the loss of stable housing. The risks and protective qualities associated with homelessness primarily focus on those living on the streets or in shelters. Further, the primary focus has been on the risks related with residential instability. Exploring the factors contributing to resilience of youth living doubled-up—an often invisible subgroup of homelessness—has the potential of informing how to support students without residential stability.

Note

1 Other federal departments, including the Department of Housing and Urban Development (HUD), have determined that living doubled-up does not qualify as homeless. Challenges associated with resource distribution have resulted in more conservative parameters. Expanding the definition would force HUD to further divide already inadequate funding and resources (National Alliance to End Homelessness, 2007). The department decided that families living doubled-up need affordable housing, not the services it provides those who live on the street and may be veterans or have a disability.

3
ENTERING THEIR LIVES AND HOMES

"Why you wanna know about us?" Isaac's stepmother, Faith, looks at me confused. "We just average people."

"That is why I am interested," I explain. "I want to know how Isaac lives his life and how that influences his education."

"Oh," she nods, "okay."

"Do you have any questions about what I am doing?" I had already reviewed the interview and observation consent forms with the family.

"No," she pauses, "I trust you."

I arrived at Isaac's apartment for our second interview. Everyone was home. "Where should we do this?" I asked. "Um," he looked at his stepbrother and two stepsisters sitting on the couch watching television, "I guess my bedroom would work." Harmony, his stepsister's daughter, was playing with a cup on the floor in his room. "You gotta go in the living room," Isaac said in a stern tone. Harmony looked up briefly, but continued playing. Isaac sighed. He carried her into the living room and asked Benjamin to make sure she stayed out of the room. Isaac shut the bedroom door and then sat on his mattress. I sat next to him while his stepsister's 2-year-old son slept between us. Throughout the interview we were interrupted by people coming in the bedroom to get things. Finding privacy in a crowded residence proved challenging.

The stories presented in the following chapters may raise the question, "How do you know this?" The process of entering the homes of doubled-up families frames how I present and understand the youth's experiences. For the most part the youth and their families found my interest in their lives curious. As Faith explained, the youth lived in neighborhoods where this residential experience was common and they viewed their lives as uninteresting. Understanding the context of my relationship with the youth sheds additional light on their residential experiences.

The overall patterns of these youth may be similar to adolescents living in urban areas across the United States. They get up each morning and follow a routine. Most attend school; some are involved in after-school activities. Evenings are spent doing homework, eating dinner and watching television. As night approaches, they get ready for bed. Weekends are less structured and involve sleepovers, parties, sports and spending time with family. All of the youth had career ambitions that required some form of postsecondary training. Although how these youth spend time sounds typical, the context where these events occur shapes how they experience the routines of life. Constructing case studies allows for analysis of the complexity and normalcy of their lives. The intent is to demonstrate how they navigate life in a doubled-up residence without a hyper-focus on the challenges they endure.

The majority of research concerning the educational experiences of homeless youth have used survey designs that highlight the magnitude of the problems homeless youth face (e.g. Ensign & Santelli, 1998; Freeman & Hamilton, 2008); however, survey methods are less useful when exploring how youth make meaning out of their residential situations. Qualitative approaches have the potential to uncover the complexity and contradictions that define the lives of homeless individuals (Duneier, 1999; Liebow, 1993). I entered the homes of the youth living doubled-up to understand how these families structured their residences. Homeless youth have complex lives, including high rates of mobility and exposure to multiple risk factors. A qualitative case study provides access to changes occurring over time, highlights how youth navigate barriers that arise, and empowers youth by allowing them to explain their lives using their own words. The next section discusses the methodology used in greater depth.

Overview of case study

Case studies are increasingly being used as a research tool by various disciplines to understand the complexity of life. A case study is defined as "a qualitative approach in which the investigator explores a bounded system (a case) or multiple bounded systems (cases) over time, through detailed, in-depth data collection involving multiple sources of information," (Creswell, 2007, p. 73). Each case is investigated within a real-life context and multiple sources of data are collected to understand each case in detail (Yin, 2003).

Case study research recognizes the importance of context in shaping social life. The holistic perspective of studying a phenomenon used in constructing a case study involves evaluating both the particular and the ordinary, but focuses on the particular (Patton, 2002; Stake, 2005). The intentional focus allows the researcher to discuss unique aspects of the case. Doubled-up residences, with at least one adolescent, in Los Angeles served as the context for this study. In chapters that follow, I share the youth's residential experiences (e.g. doing homework and getting ready for school) to illustrate how these aspects of their lives may differ from middle-class households. I explore how separate households collaborated within one residence and managed conflict between each other—issues typically not present in single-family residences.

Researchers determine the unit of analysis—the case—before entering the field (Yin, 2003). Martyn Hammersley (1992) defines a case as a "phenomenon (located in time and space) about which data are collected and/or analyzed, and that corresponds to the type of phenomena to which the main claims of the study relate" (p. 184). Data were collected from the entire residence; however, the adolescent was the primary unit of analysis. Bounding of place proves more challenging and requires reconsideration. The underlying view of space is incongruous with how mobile populations organize their lives. The residential environments of youth in this study were uncertain and changing. They had residential histories that included movement between homes, counties, states and countries. Household dynamics often shifted in unison with their residential movement. During the preliminary phase of the study—September and October 2008—I intended to collect data from four doubled-up residences living in four apartments in one housing complex. Three of the residences moved out of the complex before November 1st and I lost contact with the two that moved out of the neighborhood. The high mobility rates of doubled-up families required me to consider the fluidity of place. I identified four residences with at least one adolescent who qualified as homeless under the McKinney–Vento definition of doubled-up. Place, for the purposes of this study, had less to do with geography than the residential context. The homes and communities of the participants were primary spaces where data were collected, even if the actual apartment or neighborhood changed.

Selecting participants

The study was conducted during the 2008–9 school year. The beginning of the study happened to occur as the economic market in the United States slid into a recession. People across the country lost homes, jobs and savings. The number of families living doubled-up steadily increased. The youth in this study felt the impact of the crisis as family members lost jobs and social service programs were trimmed.

I build upon findings from an exploratory study of homeless youth and the educational process (Tierney, Gupton & Hallett, 2008). One key finding that emerged was that several different subgroups of homeless youth existed. The specific context of each subgroup influenced how they approached the educational process, resources they had available, and the educational support of their social networks. Given the importance of context, the sections below discuss the geographic location and participant section process.

Los Angeles County

Los Angeles has a larger homeless population than most states (Los Angeles Coalition to End Hunger and Homelessness, 2005). Approximately a quarter of a million individuals experience long- or short-term homelessness in the county each year (Tepper, 2004). Over 25,000 are youth and less than half attend school on a regular basis (Los Angeles Coalition to End Hunger and Homelessness, 2005). An additional 500,000 individuals live in acute poverty, which means they are one financial crisis from losing their housing (Flaming & Tepper, 2004). Many of these individuals may live in doubled-up situations and transition between other subcategories of homelessness.

Youth were selected who lived in two areas within the Los Angeles metropolitan area: Watts and Echo Park. Both are relatively small neighborhoods. According to the 2000 United States Census, approximately half of the 35,000 Watts residents live below the poverty line. The individuals living in Watts are primarily Latino (60%) and African American (40%). Nearly 40% of the residents over 25 have earned a high school diploma and 2% have completed a postsecondary degree. Approximately half of the 25,000 residents of Echo Park live below the poverty level. The demographics differ a bit: Latino (55%), African American (2%), Caucasian (14%), and Asian (25%). Table 3.1 below provides more detailed demographic information about Los Angeles County and the two areas where participants lived.

The number of families living doubled-up is difficult to approximate because government agencies do not track this residential arrangement. Although these families are covered by McKinney–Vento, they frequently are unfamiliar with the law or resources available. Lack of awareness limits the number of families living doubled-up who identify as such when registering their children at school sites. However, given the high rates of poverty and housing costs, it can be posited that rates of families living doubled-up are higher in Watts and Echo Park than more affluent areas of Los Angeles.

TABLE 3.1 Research sites—basic demographic information

	Los Angeles County	Watts	Echo Park
Population	9,948,081	34,830	25,544
Demographics:			
Caucasian	30%	<1%	14%
Latino	47%	61%	55%
African American	10%	38%	2%
Other	13%	1%	29%
Median income level	$43,518	$19,419	$30,434
Below poverty level	17%	48%	22%
Median cost of housing	$209,300	$106,325	$182,733
High school diploma or GED	70%	37%	53%
College degree	25%	2%	12%
Dropout rate	30%	63%	47%

Source: data in the above chart were taken from the 2000 Census and 2006 update (www.census.gov/census2000/states/ca.html; www.laalmanac.com/LA/la05a.htm).

Participant selection

I selected four adolescents as the primary focus of this study. Table 3.2 outlines basic demographic information of the participants. During the initial visit to each residence, I asked him or her to describe the layout of the home, where each person slept, and verified the financial necessity of the living arrangement. This information was used to confirm each youth's status as doubled-up. I chose four residences because this gave me the ability to dedicate one day per week to each as well as the flexibility to attend events (e.g. parties and soccer games) as they arose.

Selecting youth between the ages of 16 and 17 was purposeful. They were at the crossroads between childhood and adulthood. Adolescents can articulate how they understand their past and future more clearly than younger children. In addition, youth drop out at higher rates during middle school and high school than at any other point in the educational process (Berliner et al., 2008). Initially, I included two youth who were 14 years of age. Preliminary interviews revealed that they did not have enough time in school to establish relationships or an academic record. Their responsibilities to the household and perceptions also differed significantly from those nearing adulthood. Four youth were selected for the final analysis; however, informal interviews and observations were conducted with members of their residences, along with friends and members of their social network outside of the household.

TABLE 3.2 Research participants—basic demographic information

	Isaac	Kylee	Marco	Juan
Race and ethnicity	Biracial (Black and Mexican American)	Biracial (Black and Mexican American)	Mexican American	Salvadorian American
Age	17	16	17	17
Grade	10th grade	11th grade	12th grade	12th grade
Area of Los Angeles	Watts	Watts	Watts	Echo Park
People in household	10–12	7	7	8
Households represented	4	2	2	3
Residence	Three-bedroom house	Three-bedroom apartment	Three-bedroom house	Two-bedroom apartment
Participant's space	Shared room with father and adult sister	Shared room with two siblings and two children of roommate	Shared room with stepbrother and adult roommate	Shared room with mother, two siblings. He slept in the closet

Identifying youth who were willing and eligible to participate in the study proved to be a challenge. These youth were highly mobile and tended to be invisible to school systems (Tierney & Hallett, 2010). The youth did not readily identify as doubled-up when interacting with peers, teachers or school staff. Most had not even heard the term before. Programs or school organizations, such as those for undocumented or foster youth, did not exist for homeless or doubled-up youth at the school sites. The invisibility of this subpopulation of students and the internalized sense of shame created barriers to access. For example, Kylee recommended that I speak to one of her friends about participating in the study. Her friend was interested in the gift card given as compensation, but told Kylee that she "don't want him to see my house. I don't know what he might say." I spoke with her friend a few times while observing Kylee and she later expressed an interest in the study; however, I had already selected participants at that time.

Two methods of identifying participants were used. First, I established a relationship with a family living doubled-up in Watts during a previous research project (see Tierney, Gupton & Hallett, 2008). Isaac, a member of that residence, agreed to participate and his family introduced me to Kylee, who lived in the same apartment complex at that time. Second, I contacted two youth, Marco and Juan, who participated in a mentoring program through the research center where I worked. I explained what I intended to do and assured them that declining would not impact their involvement in the mentoring program. Both agreed to participate. I explained the study to each residence during my first visit. After reviewing the goals and procedures, I encouraged youth and family members to ask questions. Youth were provided a $10 gift card; I explained that not answering a specific question or asking to end the interview would not influence compensation.

Entering other people's space

Many studies of resilience involve surveys. Context is absent. Considering how context shapes resilience is a relatively new area of research. Interaction between the youth and environment may be important when determining the importance of risk and protective factors (Seidman & Pedersen, 2003). The holistic, individual-in-context perspective questions the dominant canon—searching for universal laws. I entered doubled-up homes in an attempt to observe how youth navigated life and to hear their stories. Instead of identifying a list of risk and protective factors, I wanted to understand why and how these factors functioned.

Gathering their experiences

The lives of these youth were complex and frequently changed. Meeting on a regular basis with the family allowed me to establish relationships that made my presence less awkward. I initially planned two observations per month with each youth, but shortly after entering their homes I realized this design was inadequate.

Consistent interactions were needed to establish a trusting relationship. So, I visited with each youth at least once a week. Observations were conducted throughout the project, but transitioned between two phases.

During the first phase I primarily spent time with youth in or around their residence after school hours. After they got used to my presence, I joined whatever plans they had for the day. I helped with homework and college applications. I also played games, watched television and ate meals. At times, I just "kicked it" with the youth on their porch or the street corner. As I transitioned into the second phase, I asked youth to allow me to visit locations where they spent time outside of the home. This involved attending sporting events and parties, visiting the homes of friends, and meeting extended family. I also continued spending time in the youth's residence, because they generally spent the majority of their out-of-school hours at home. Although youth spoke about "illicit acts" (e.g. gang involvement and drug use), I never observed those activities firsthand.

The process differed with Juan. The structure of his household limited my access to his residence. His aunt refused to allow me access to the apartment where his family lived, but he agreed to participate in interviews and invited me to observe him outside the residence (i.e. soccer games, walking home and a campus visit). I asked him detailed questions about the residence, had him draw a picture of the physical space, and allowed him to read and edit my description of the apartment.

Detailed field notes were written after each visit as it was difficult to take notes while observing. The youth did not mind participating in the study, but felt uncomfortable if I wrote while we were spending time together. Marco, for example, was showing me an essay he was writing for a scholarship. I took notes about our conversation and wrote a physical description of the bedroom. He asked what I was doing. I explained. He looked at me with one eyebrow raised, "That's weird." After an awkward pause, I put my notebook away and our conversation returned to his essay. From that point on I occasionally wrote down a word or quote that could be used to jog my memory, but did not want extensive note-taking to disrupt the environment. I then drafted a brief summary shortly after getting into my car to guide my memory when constructing detailed notes at home.

Collecting their stories

Interviews helped me paint a clear picture of each person and analyze contradictions that existed between actions and perceptions. The youth participated in three semi-structured interviews. Interviews, lasting approximately one hour, were digitally recorded and generally occurred in the youth's residence. The first interview focused on outlining their residential histories, educational backgrounds and social networks, whereas the second interview clarified risk and protective factors identified during the first round of interviews and observations. I had two goals during the second interview. Youth were asked specific questions based upon observations. Then I presented them with a preliminary social network web. They were asked if the web included all the people they spent a significant amount of time with over the previous six months. After reviewing the list of individuals, I asked for a description of each person and an occasion when they spent time together. The third interview involved clarifying details of their lives and how they understood their residential situation. I also gave each youth a copy of vignettes, presented in Chapters 4 to 7, and allowed them to comment.[1]

Family members and others who influenced the youth's educational choices (e.g. peers or mentors) participated in semi-structured interviews. These interviews or conversations were not digitally recorded, but I took extensive notes. In general, I approached the person of interest with specific questions related to the youth or emerging themes. Marco's cousin participated in several short interviews. The purpose was to understand how he discussed college with Marco. I also conducted interviews with individuals who had information concerning the residence when the youth was unaware of the details. Kylee's mother explained her decision to move her children into a doubled-up residence.

Reviewing supporting materials

I was given access to a variety of documents that helped clarify data collected using other methods, including high school transcripts, letters from colleges and homework assignments. At times I asked for a document to verify information (e.g. high school transcripts for a youth's grade point average), and at other times a member of the residence solicited my assistance understanding a form or letter. Isaac's stepmother asked me to help her understand the terms of an eviction notice and letters sent from the school district concerning her children's attendance.

As my relationship with the residence developed, I offered to assist with homework and college applications. Marco and Juan asked me to review essays they had written for college scholarships. Kylee and her sister, who was in middle school, brought questions they had about their homework. Kylee's mother also asked me for help writing an essay for a community college course she was taking. She handed me a folder with all of her graded papers and asked me to review an essay titled 'My Ideal Roommate' in which she had written about her experiences living as a doubled-up mother.

The role of trust

Throughout the research process I was forced to evaluate my own perceptions. To what extent was I projecting my own experiences on these youth? How well did I actually understand their lives? And, what was my role? Growing up in a low-income community increased my comfort level in their homes and communities. Issues of race and family structure separated us, but living in crowded residences with few resources created a common bond. At two points during childhood my parents sought refuge in the home of a family member after a financial crisis.

We also had family members move into our home when they were unable to afford to live independently. I remember how crowded conditions led to conflict over space. I also fondly remember playing with cousins outside or telling jokes when we were supposed to be sleeping.

I typically do not divulge too much information about my past during the research process unless participants ask. Spending a significant amount of time in the youth's homes with their families often led to conversations about my life and views. Just as I was interested in their lives, they found my presence in Watts to be peculiar and fascinating. In each home I was asked why a White guy with a college degree would spend time in their neighborhood. Sharing my background helped my presence make sense and increased their comfort level. Discussing my own experiences often led to more intimate conversations. After I discussed my experiences sharing a bedroom with my cousins and sister, Kylee felt comfortable showing me her bedroom.

Similarities in residential history brought me closer to the youth, but I did not assume the role of an insider. Aspects of our lives differed. These differences at times created challenges to understanding each other. Slang used in the urban communities confused me at times. When I saw the word "crushing" written on the hand of Kylee's friend I thought it was a reference to fighting, but actually it referred to having a crush on someone. Several times I had to ask for a translation of terms. We also perceived the police and government differently. Admittedly, I recognize that both institutions have issues that need to be addressed, but I believe the majority of people in public service are genuinely good people. The youth generally feared and loathed police.

My role in the lives of the participants differed. All four of the youth saw me as a resource, but in different ways. Isaac and Kylee enjoyed my company. They were not interested in my attempts to encourage them to participate in school and consider going to college. They liked spending time with me watching television or joking around. Kylee also enjoyed walking me around the neighborhood and introducing me to her friends. Marco and Juan were more strategic. They took advantage of the time we spent together to ask questions about attending college and filling out forms. One aspect of the study that I had not anticipated was meeting youth who had some sense of my role as a researcher and wanted me to share their voice. I felt a deep sense of commitment to present their stories accurately and find a platform to share their opinions about their families, schools and communities.

Throughout the data collection stages youth were given the opportunity to respond to my understanding of the data. I took steps to enable the participants to reflect on how I presented them. The youth agreed that I captured the essence of their story, or at least the part that I had asked about and they had been willing to share. Member checks gave participants the opportunity to correct errors and respond to my interpretation of their lives. The youth made minor corrections, but the general consensus was that I had described each of them accurately. Isaac laughed while reading his portion of the chapter:

RONN: What is so funny?

ISAAC: How did you know I was thinking that?

RONN: I pay close attention to what you do and then take notes. I also compare that to what you said in the interviews.

ISAAC: It is good. You could be a writer.

RONN: I am a writer.

ISAAC: No, a real writer, like one that writes books. People would want to read this stuff.

RONN: I am writing a book.

ISAAC: I mean, like a real book that people would want to read.

RONN: I'll try.

ISAAC: Good.

Note

1 I should note that I did not allow Kylee or Isaac to review my analysis concerning the likelihood of their academic failure. We spoke about the risks they faced and I offered advice, but I did not feel comfortable telling a teenager that I predicted his or her failure. I hoped they would prove me wrong.

PART I
Separate Households

Separate households involved residences where individuals and families lived alongside each other without collaborating. As will be discussed further in later chapters, this arrangement negatively influenced the youth's educational participation. Living in a separate household did not guarantee that an individual would disengage from the educational process, but it was a risk factor. The residential structure and social network of each participant worked together to influence educational resilience. In this section I share the experiences of two youth living in separate residences— Isaac and Juan. Each chapter begins with background information before providing a "day in the life" of each student and analysis of factors encouraging either risk or protection.

4

ISAAC'S LONG SHOT

"What do you want to be?" I ask one afternoon.

"I want to play basketball," Isaac pauses, "but if basketball doesn't work out, I want to work for the fire department."

"How is that going to happen for you?" I inquire.

"I need to finish school and try to go to college," he sighs. "I am going to try."

Baggy, black athletic gear covers Isaac's thin frame. He stands 5'11" and tells people he is Black, but his father is Mexican American. He has the beginnings of a mustache and large brown eyes. He saves eye contact for only his closest friends and family. I knew his stepbrother for nearly a year before Isaac would say more than a few words in front of me.

Isaac's family experienced a series of events in short succession that led to his residential instability. Throughout elementary school, he lived with his mother and stepfather. After they separated, he moved with his mother into a two-bedroom apartment with his grandmother and aunt. His residential stability further deteriorated when his mother was sent to prison. "I think she did a robbery in Texas and then they caught her out here." His voice softens when he speaks about personal issues. "There was a warrant, they took her back to Texas." His grandmother briefly took over parenting responsibilities. He takes a deep breath, "me and my grandma wasn't really getting along, so she ended up getting me in [foster care] placement. She said she wouldn't take care of me because I wasn't listening to her."

Isaac transitioned between several foster care placements before being reunited with an extended family member who currently serves as his guardian. Faith, the mother of his cousin's girlfriend, became his foster parent and gained custody with reduced supervision because she had a "family" connection—Faith's daughter was dating Isaac's cousin. The residents of his house represent four different households. Faith, her two sons, daughter and Isaac comprise one household; Faith's oldest daughter, her boyfriend and their two children represent another; and two adult males each are their own household unit. Ricardo, a friend Faith met while living in a hotel downtown, is an undocumented 50-year-old man who works two full-time jobs to make ends meet. The other man, David, has a 3-year-old son, but the relationship with his son's mother is complicated. She was 16 and he was 23 when their baby was born, which led to a felony conviction.

The residents share a three-bedroom house in Watts (see Figure 4.1). The main room includes a kitchen and living room with two couches, sitting perpendicular, that face away from the front door. Bits of food, soiled clothes and other items cover the dingy white tile floor. Dirty dishes, school binders, thawing meat, noodles, among other things, teeter precariously on the dining room table. The trash can is nearly buried in overflowing garbage. Faith's bedroom has clothes and other items piled waist high with a path to her mattress that sits on the floor. The boys' room has two mattresses that are stacked during the day, but are laid out and shared at night. Another bedroom has one double bed and a small mattress that Africa pulls out. The tub in the main bathroom no longer works; the toilet seat remains attached by one screw. Everyone now shares the master bathroom.

Isaac and the residents allowed me to visit whenever I desired. My presence was requested when navigating bureaucracies, including a visit to the social security

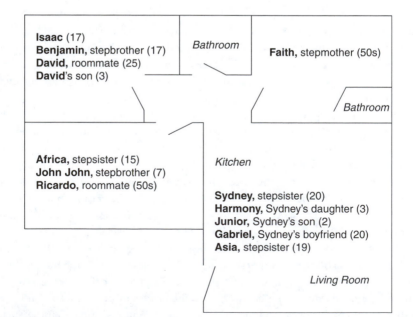

FIGURE 4.1 Isaac's house

office and meeting with school officials. Isaac also allowed me to follow him when he went to his friends' homes.

A day in the life of Isaac

Morning

"Hurry up, we already late," Faith pulls her 7-year-old son, John John, along the sidewalk by his left hand while his other hand rubs the sleep from his eyes. They arrive at the elementary school ten minutes late. The attendance clerk greets Faith by name; it is their morning ritual. She hands John John a late slip and encourages Faith to arrive on time tomorrow. "I know, these kids is lazy," Faith throws her hands in the air. John John slowly walks down the hall with his Spider-Man back-pack hanging lopsided from his narrow shoulders. Two weeks' worth of unfinished homework is crumpled in his backpack. As Faith walks home she worries that the school will report her again. Last year the district filed a complaint because John John and Africa, her 15-year-old daughter, missed 90 days of school and Benjamin, her 17-year-old son, had not been enrolled for 3 years.

When she gets back to the house her 17-year-old stepson, Isaac, is lounging on the couch watching the morning news. He was unable to watch the Lakers play last night because the cable was shut off a month ago. He hopes to catch the score and maybe a few highlights. The professional players in Los Angeles inspire and entertain him. Isaac aspires to be the next Kobe Bryant. Although never part of an official basketball team, Isaac takes advantage of every opportunity to play. The possibility of playing basketball at the collegiate level is his only motivation for completing high school. Harmony and Junior, his oldest stepsister's two children, are sleeping on the other couch. Their mother left the house nearly two months ago with a new boyfriend.

Faith walks toward her bedroom as Africa comes out of the bathroom. "You better go to school today," Faith points her finger at Africa. "I ain't gonna go to that school again for a meeting." "I was planning on it," Africa yells without looking at her mother, "You don't need to tell me." Faith slams her bedroom door and turns on a Spanish music station. Africa pulls her short hair back and uses a rubber band to secure the ponytail. She comes out of the bedroom with a white polo shirt tucked into her tight blue Capri pants. "Where's my binder?" she asks to no one in particular. Isaac shrugs, "I don't know, it ain't mine." Africa glares at him as she digs through the heap of dirty dishes, food and random items covering the kitchen table, "Here it is." She wipes peanut butter off the top of it and leaves without saying goodbye. Nonchalantly she walks to school. First period ends soon. She plans to arrive as classes switch and sneak in unnoticed … or maybe she will just spend the day with a friend. Africa turns in the direction of her friend's house.

Isaac continues watching television. He has no plans for the day. His stepsisters' two young children are now awake. He ignores them. Junior picks up bits of food from the floor and table to eat and Harmony, who wet her pants while sleeping, now plays with Benjamin's black sneakers that were left by the couch. Junior finds a glass half full of Coke on the table and eagerly begins to drink. Harmony drops the shoes when she hears her brother gulp and runs over to where he is standing. He screams as she grabs the glass from him. They struggle. Junior hits his sister's arm and she loses her grip. Shards of glass land next to their bare feet. Faith opens her bedroom door, "What are you doing? You need to go sit on the couch, now." The two kids look at her without moving. "You kids make me crazy. Someone need to clean that mess." Faith slams the door before finishing the last word. Isaac stands, picks up the large pieces of glass and places them in the trash. The kids continue to play with the soda that spilled as he sits back on the couch.

After an hour he gets up and looks through the kitchen for something to eat. He stares at the shelves in the refrigerator, but most of the food is either spoiled or frozen. He returns to the couch without eating. Benjamin comes out of their bedroom around 9:00 and flops on the other couch. They watch *Good Morning America* without talking. Junior falls asleep next to Benjamin; Harmony entertains herself with a broom and sock. Faith joins them around 9:30. "Faith, I need to go to the school to register," Isaac says in a soft voice. She sighs as she sits down, "You kids always been needing something. I ain't going with you this time, I got things to do." "But I think you need to sign the forms," Isaac protests. "I ain't got time today," Faith leans her head back on the couch and rubs her temples. "Maybe tomorrow." Isaac goes in his room to get his sweatshirt. She has promised three times in the past two weeks to take him to register. Faith is sitting with her back to the front door as he opens it. He tries to shut the door quietly behind him, but the knob is broken and it needs to be slammed. Faith yells, "Where you going?" Isaac does not respond; he knows she will not chase after him.

Daytime

Isaac walks up the driveway towards Tim Tim who is under the hood of a car. His house sits next to his grandmother's home, which is known as the candy house because neighbors come by to purchase sodas, chips and other snacks she has purchased at the grocery store and sells at a slightly inflated price. Tim Tim runs a small automotive repair business out of his garage. "What up LS," he walks over and they "dap" – an elaborate handshake between friends. Isaac acquired the nickname "Little Slayer" or "LS" while living downtown in Skid Row. His cousin, Gabriel, is known as "Slayer," a reference to his gang activities. It is tradition for older men to have younger protégés take their name. They talk for a few minutes and then Tim Tim leans over the engine, "Why don't you go into house. I will come in after I finish here."

Isaac goes through the front door. He turns on the PlayStation, sits on the couch and lights a cigarette as the latest NBA game loads. Isaac selects the Lakers, of course, as the home team; today he will play against the Clippers. Intra-city rivalry is always fun. Tim Tim comes in the house a few minutes later. "What team you wanna lose with today?" Tim Tim asks as he scrubs the grease off his hands at the kitchen sink. "Whatever," Isaac slowly exhales smoke, "I can beat you with any team." The two play the video game for an hour. Around noon two members of Tim Tim's gang, a rival of Gabriel's group, come over. The taller of the two looks at the television, "Why you always playing on TV when we can play for reals?" They decide to play two on two in the driveway. Isaac and Tim Tim barely win a 21 to 19 point game. Isaac's stomach growls; he does not say anything. He eats when his friend offers, which rarely happens, but will not ask for food because he is too proud and does not want to jeopardize his welcome.

The four men go into the house. Isaac and the shorter of the two men sit on the couch and watch ESPN as Tim Tim escorts the other man into the bedroom. Isaac knows not to ask. He assumes they are discussing drugs or gang activity. A few minutes later the men exit the bedroom. "Let's roll," announces the taller man who has a new bulge in his front coat pocket. Isaac looks in their direction and nods, "Peace." Tim Tim returns to the garage. Isaac sits on the couch for a few more minutes. He is bored. He could go home, but there is nothing going on over there either. His stomach growls again. He stands and walks out the front door. "Later," he waves in Tim Tim's direction.

Evening

Isaac walks the block home from Tim Tim's. A golden brown dog with matted hair and a limp eats trash in the gutter, but pauses to growl as Isaac nears. Isaac quickens his pace without taking his eye off the dog. John John and Benjamin are tossing a football in the driveway while Harmony pushes Junior in a stroller that now serves as a toy. Junior yells "Hey"—the only word he knows—as he spots Isaac walking towards the house. Isaac opens the front door without pausing to talk. Africa looks up from the couch but returns to painting her fingernails neon green. He goes into his bedroom, sits on a mattress and takes a deep breath. A few minutes later, John John comes into the room, "Hey, you wanna play basketball?" Isaac stands, "Yeah, but you gonna lose." He follows John John out the front door and around the house. Isaac rigs a basketball hoop out of a blue crate and piece of wood they find in the alley. John John looks for the basketball they received during a church outreach last month.

The two play for a while, but John John is no match for Isaac. At dusk they head into the house—Isaac does not feel safe outside after dark. Faith, Benjamin and Africa are sitting on the couches watching a police drama on television. Junior eats an orange and throws pieces of the peel on the floor. "Can I cook one of these," Isaac points to a mound of pork chops thawing uncovered on the table. "I don't care," Faith waves him off.

Isaac fries a pork chop and boils broccoli. John John finds a skillet on the table and scrapes the remnants from a previous meal on the floor. "Be careful," Faith orders as she heads toward her room, "Africa, you watch him." John John stands on his tiptoes as he pours oil into the pan before lighting the gas stove with a match. The egg sizzles as it hits the skillet. Isaac sits on the couch with his meal. "Are you done with the pan," Africa asks. Isaac nods. "Hey, will you make me some?" Benjamin asks. "I guess," Africa pauses, "but you need to gets me some candy." They agree that he will purchase Now or Laters from the candy store—two green and one red.

Isaac rinses his plate and finds a place to put it on the haphazard stack of dishes in the sink before returning to the couch. Faith comes out of the bedroom with her boyfriend, Mario, who had been taking a nap in the bedroom. Mario began frequenting the apartment about a month again. Isaac does not trust Mario, a 25-year-old with a reputation of sleeping with women in the neighborhood willing to buy him liquor. Faith pauses at the front door, "You kids need to cleans this place." Faith attempts to shut the door twice before leaving it ajar and walking down the driveway with Mario.

Africa finishes frying the pork chops and, after making a plate for herself, looks at Benjamin, "It's done." Benjamin gets food and sits back on the couch. Harmony and Junior alternate between coming over for a piece of meat and playing with a few Christmas bulbs that have remained out. Harmony begins dancing in a circle and sings make-believe words progressively louder until Africa responds, "Shut up." Harmony pauses and then launches the red ornament she is holding, which shatters against the wall. "You're so bad," Africa looks at her in disgust, but no one cleans up the shards of glass.

Around 8:30, Ricardo comes home from work. "Hey, Ricardo," John John waves, but no one else acknowledges Ricardo's presence. He quickly makes a Cup-O-Noodles before going to bed. He needs to leave for work by 5:00 tomorrow morning. Working two jobs, seven days a week, and traveling by public transportation limits the amount of time Ricardo spends in the house.

At 10:00 Isaac goes into the bedroom to lie down. Faith returns a couple of minutes later. She spent the last few hours drinking with Mario down the block. "I need to get up early tomorrow," he tells himself. He expects her to be angry in the morning when the hangover sets in. Africa and Benjamin stay up for several more hours watching television. Harmony and Junior fall asleep on one of the couches; they have learned to sleep through the noise. As midnight approaches everyone has found a place to sleep.

Weekend

The weekend starts like any other day of the week. Isaac lounges around his bedroom bantering with Benjamin. Tonight, however, Isaac plans to attend a party at his friend's house. He met Prince when he lived in South Central—two residences ago. Prince works as a housekeeper at a hotel and hosts a party once every two weeks when he gets paid. In general, guests pay $2 or $3 to help cover the cost of food and alcohol. Isaac and a few select others receive free admission.

At 2:00 in the afternoon Isaac begins preparing for the party. He makes certain that he has clean clothes and irons an oversized plain black T-shirt. With a wet paper towel he washes the marks off of his Michael Jordan basketball shoes. He prepares in his room with the door shut. Sydney, who spent six weeks in Las Vegas, returned last night after realizing that money was no longer being deposited into her welfare account. The balance on her welfare card reached zero. She arrived last night begging Faith to allow her to move back into the house and promised to deal with her substance abuse problem. Benjamin and Sydney argued all night about her being an alcoholic and him not wanting her around anymore. Isaac does not want to get involved in a fight. He tries to avoid conflict by staying in his room or leaving the house.

Isaac's bedroom door swings open. Benjamin flops on one of the mattresses after slamming the door, "That girl is crazy. She gots some psychological problems." Isaac shakes his head, "That's why I ain't messing with her." Until recently Isaac spent most of his free time with Sydney, who has been dating his cousin, Gabriel, for several years. Gabriel joined a gang two years ago and recruited Isaac. Isaac went to a few gatherings, but the guns and violence made him nervous. He confided in Gabriel that he wanted out. Unfortunately, it was not that easy. Since he recruited Isaac, Gabriel was responsible for deactivation and initiated a fight with Isaac while three other members assisted in holding arms and throwing punches. The event created a rift between Isaac and Gabriel. Since Sydney and Gabriel are romantically involved and have two children together, she also gives Isaac a hard time.

Isaac gathers his things and leaves the house without notifying anyone of his intended destination or when he will return. He sees Sydney walking down the street in front of him. Harmony pulls away from her mother and yells, "I don't wanna." Sydney slaps her daughter's face, "Stop crying now." Tears form in Harmony's eyes. Sydney plans to spend the weekend in a hotel with friends to celebrate her return. Everyone will pool money for liquor, marijuana and ecstasy. Harmony will be expected to entertain herself and not get in the way. Isaac walks a few blocks to a different bus stop.

He arrives at Prince's house a little before 6:00. Prince's father is sitting on the couch watching television, "Hey LS." "What up," Isaac nods. Prince's parents allow parties as long as they are invited to participate. Isaac walks down the hall to Prince's bedroom where two young men sit on the couch in the corner drinking a beer. Prince gets off the couch, "What up LS?" He hands Isaac a beer. For a small fee, his parents purchase alcohol for their son's parties. Isaac sits on the floor, opens the beer, and looks up at Prince, "You got a cig?" Prince opens his pack, "Here ya go." One of the other guys opens a small bag of marijuana and rolls a blunt—a paper used for homemade cigarettes filled with marijuana. Several blunts are passed around the room over the next hour. Isaac takes a drag each time it reaches him as well as smoking half a pack of cigarettes and drinking a six-pack of beer. Isaac already feels buzzed before the party officially starts.

A steady stream of people arrives between 9:00 and 10:00. The backyard and living room serve as the overflow after the bedroom fills to capacity. Prince sits next to the front door and collects the $2 cover charge. He shares a blunt with his father as his mother fills a bowl with chips. Isaac and Prince's father play basketball on the PlayStation in the living room; Isaac wants to sober up a bit before he ends up puking. A loud thump is followed by a female voice yelling outside, "You fucking bitch, I'm gonna beat your ass." Prince pulls up the window blinds, "Oh shit." Two women standing inches apart yell at each other and wildly wave their arms. Prince runs outside. Well aware that a few people have brought weapons, Isaac nervously watches from the window. The shorter woman pushes the other woman's arm, "Get your hand outta my face." The taller woman drops her purse and lunges. Prince squeezes between them, "Either knock this shit off or get out." "What's goin' on out there?" his dad yells from the couch. "Nothin'," Prince returns his attention to the women. The taller of the two pauses before turning to her friend, "Fuck this, let's go." As they walk through the gate and into the alley, people return to their conversations.

After the party settles down, Isaac decides to leave in order to catch the last bus of the night. He says goodbye to people in the bedroom. Down the block from his friend's house, he sits with his head in his hands and forces his eyes open to keep the bus stop from spinning. He climbs the two steps onto the bus and chooses a seat away from the five other passengers. The bus ride takes 20 minutes. The high he felt at the party evaporates as he walks three blocks to his house with great concentration and a heightened sense of his surroundings. Slowly he opens the door to his house; he does not want to wake Harmony and Junior. Isaac lies on his mattress without changing clothes and quickly falls asleep.

Reflecting on risk and protective factors

A shy individual by nature, Isaac hated moving and meeting new people. He longed for a stable living environment and his own space. Unfortunately, the majority of his life involved mobility and instability. Unlike the other youth, Isaac was disengaged from the educational process. His daily routines drew him further from school as the study progressed. He aspired to earn a degree or credential from a postsecondary institution, but took few steps towards realizing that goal.

Residential history and context

Isaac went through a series of short-term placements involving foster and group homes after his mother was extradited to Texas for a five-year prison sentence. A social worker tried to reunite him with his grandmother and an aunt, but both attempts failed. Isaac had run away from each of their homes and neither wanted the added responsibility of dealing with a teenager. The final family member contacted by Child and Family Services (CFS) was his cousin, Gabriel, who lived with Faith. Since Gabriel was only 18 years old he was unable to take custody. Being that Faith was the grandmother of Gabriel's children, CFS granted her "family privileges" that allowed sidestepping typical requirements for foster placement. After a three-month trial, Faith received permanent guardianship even though the school had filed educational neglect complaints concerning three of her children. "I think of Faith like a mom, but I don't call her mom. I feel shy. I know that she not my mom and I can't go around calling somebody else 'mom.' I think of her like that though." His birth mother had been released from prison a few months before the study began; however, CFS determined that she could not regain custody until she had proof of a stable job and residence. A terminal illness requiring chemotherapy that surfaced during her prison term complicated her ability to pursue work.

The family lived in four residences in three years. Initially, he moved to the Skid Row hotel where Faith stayed with her children. "The rooms are small in there, like the people in there don't really take care of their hygiene. It's nasty, the bathroom is nasty." The entire family moved to a three-bedroom apartment in South Central Los Angeles with a roommate, Ricardo, who offered to help pay rent. Three households—Faith and her children; her oldest daughter, her boyfriend, and their two children; and the roommate—lived in the unit for nine months before they were evicted. The eviction notice stated the family violated the rental agreement by not taking care of the apartment. Another roommate, David, joined the residence when the family moved to an apartment in Watts. Another eviction notice arrived 11 months later and a month into this study. The letter stated that the family was not taking care of the home, the number of residents exceeded the contract, and the family played music too loudly. They moved a block away to a three-bedroom house sitting on a plot with two other houses. The front house was occupied by the landlord and the two back houses were rental units. "This is my first house really staying in," Isaac grinned, "This is better than the apartment, cause the apartment was smaller and this one has more space. We can go outside and the manager doesn't complain. I just have more freedom."

The uncertainty concerning who was going to live in the residence each month made space distribution and financial contributions difficult to manage. Rent was $1,500. David and Ricardo each contributed $200, Sydney paid $250, and Faith covered the final $850. However, rental contributions were never certain. David moved out permanently in January and Sydney disappeared for weeks at a time leaving Faith with Sydney's two children, $450 short of the rental payment, and a landlord who charged $50 each day rent was late. Faith was unable to pay the full amount for rent in March. In moments of crisis the residents worked together out of desperation: Benjamin met with his pastor, Africa called her older sister, and Faith contacted the welfare office. Benjamin and John John placed charcoal in a hole they dug behind the house to heat up meals after the gas, electric and water companies discontinued services in February.

Communication frequently broke down either to fighting or avoidance. The already contentious relationships within the residence further deteriorated as economic problems mounted.

Childcare was the responsibility of each mother. When Sydney left town to live with a new boyfriend in Las Vegas, her children were left in the household. No one consistently supervised Harmony and Junior; the residents simply dealt with their presence and expressed frustration with Sydney's lack of accountability. Faith was responsible for her children and Isaac, but she rarely monitored behavior. Isaac had freedom to come and go as he saw fit, and explained that "Every now and again Faith will be asking me what time I be coming home, but mostly she doesn't." The unsanitary conditions served as evidence of the lack of collaboration. Isaac was frustrated that an attempt made by a social worker to bring order to the home failed:

> We used to have [a cleaning schedule] but it didn't work out. People wasn't doing it when they was supposed to. Like Tuesday I clean the bathroom and Africa have the living room that whole day and Sydney has the kitchen and Benjamin has to sweep the floor or something. Everybody wasn't doing their part.

The residence was plagued by conflict. Each household and resident had equal footing; however, avoidance and abuse were employed more often than conflict resolution. "Everyone always be fighting here," Isaac explained, "That's why I leave." When a conflict could not be resolved between residents, it often escalated because no authority figure or arbitrator existed to manage disputes. Faith avoided conflict. Isaac felt that her attempts at discipline were arbitrary and he knew she would not follow through on threats. I got the sense that he wanted structure and discipline, but that desire eroded as he got used to independence.

In April, Faith received notice that her family would be evicted again. Ricardo, frustrated by the constant fighting and numerous evictions, did not want to continue being part of the residence. Faith told her 18-year-old son, Benjamin, and Isaac that she was going to find a one-bedroom apartment to live in with Africa and John John. The two boys, uncertain if Faith would follow through on the threat, searched for other residential options. Since neither of the boys had a high school diploma or work experience, both planned to move into a Skid Row hotel where they could earn an income through welfare programs and illegal activities.

Social network

Isaac's social network included few high school or college graduates. When I asked if he knew anyone who went to college, he paused and looked at me, "I know you." His parents and stepparent dropped out of high school and none of the residents of his current home attended school regularly except his 7-year-old stepbrother. His 19-year-old stepsister, Asia, attended a community college, but he rarely saw her after she moved in with a mentor and enrolled in a college preparation charter school. Asia spent weekends and holidays in the residence. "I see her sometimes, but she think she better than us. I don't really like talking to her," Isaac explained. He generally left the house when she visited.

Isaac spent the majority of time with Prince and Tim Tim, both of whom had gang connections and provided him with drugs and alcohol. The weekend after Isaac's birthday, his friends pooled money to pay for a hotel room near downtown Los Angeles. He spent five days drinking alcohol, smoking pot and using ecstasy with Prince, Gabriel and two of Isaac's stepsisters. "We just hung and watched TV and stuff," Isaac shared. His girlfriend at the time, a 27-year-old drug dealer, also stayed in the hotel to celebrate his 17th birthday. Two days after the party ended she was arrested. "She was selling drugs downtown and doing them. I didn't do them. She ain't really my girlfriend anyways," Isaac laughed, "She's just some girl that likes me." She spent a few weeks in jail, but was given a short sentence since it was her first arrest. "She crazy, she call me all the time," he shook his head. "What a 27-year-old be doing messing with a 17-year-old?" Isaac avoided her most of the time. However, he was lured into spending time with her because she provided him with money, drugs and alcohol.

Saturdays during the summer and fall he played basketball with a social service organization in Skid Row. Teams of three played a series of games before playoffs each December. The goal of the program was to provide an opportunity to do something positive for men living in or near Skid Row. In addition to playing ball, the league commissioner, a former gang member, wanted to "teach these guys about life." Each week began with a word of the day—such as teamwork or determination. The commissioner had a vision for using the league to address apathy and gang violence. The guys joked that "LS," Isaac's street name, stood for "Little Shooter." The program gave Isaac something to look forward to each week. "I think [my team] might win the championship this time." The time spent in Skid Row also helped foster his relationships with drug dealers and gang members after he left the basketball court, including the woman who claimed to be his girlfriend.

Educational factors

The majority of Isaac's time in foster care did not include school attendance. He initially was placed in a series of group homes, but he ran away several times. I asked him why he moved so frequently. Isaac explained:

> The fosters, uh, sometimes in different foster homes or group homes I get into a fight with different people or either the foster mom, she would kick me out or I would have to go somewhere else. When I was in Palmdale and San Fernando, I didn't like staying there cause it was far and I didn't know nobody there. And then, like, most of the time the group home didn't have food, so they keep your allowance and don't give it to you.

He was not enrolled in school the entire time he was in the foster care system. After missing school for nearly three years, Isaac enrolled in an independent study program in the fall of 2007, which required attendance twice a week for an hour to turn in packets and take tests. A social worker assisted him with registering for the program. Motivated students completed two years of coursework in one year. Isaac moved from zero credits to sophomore status. Although he had a 2.5 GPA and attended school regularly, Isaac felt he was missing his opportunity to be on a high school basketball team. His mentor helped him enroll in a charter school during the summer of 2008. Isaac stopped going to school after three days. He was frustrated by rules restricting his ability to play sports. "I wanted to play on a basketball team, but the coach said transfers were not allowed to play," he shrugged, "I don't know." His mentor spoke with the coach and got an exception to the rule; however, Isaac was no longer eligible because of poor grades and attendance.

A school district representative, Ms Black, stopped by the house in January after he missed five months of school. She explained that he needed to enroll in school or Faith's guardianship would be terminated and he would be moved to a group home for foster youth. Isaac agreed to attend an alternative school that offered general education courses in the morning and job training each afternoon. "I can get all the paperwork together," Ms Black sternly spoke to Isaac, "I will pick you and Faith up on Thursday at 8:00 to enroll. Make sure you are ready; we cannot be late." Faith and Isaac were both awake and ready. The departure time came and went. Isaac gave up at 9:00 and went to Tim Tim's house. He did not attend school during the final few months of the school year.

School was not an expectation in Isaac's residence. His stepsister missed school three to four times a week. Faith explained that Africa was "hanging out with this girl who got a reputation and now Africa is, how do you say, famous with the boys." His stepbrother dropped out of school in 8th grade. Isaac's lack of school attendance went unnoticed. "I haven't been in school cause the school I was in I kinda didn't like. And then I was supposed to go to a home school, but. … " Isaac shrugged.

Isaac did not have contact with teachers. The most recent encounter was four months before the study began when he was enrolled in the independent study school. His education program was supervised by Ms K; he described his relationship with her:

> I really didn't communicate with her unless I wanted to do a test or some-thing, she would give it to me. Other than that I would not really ask her no questions. Most of the time when I went in I had a package finished, so I usually took my test, usually the whole hour. She sat, she graded, and mostly she was on her computer. By the time I finished with my test it be time to go home.

He had inconsistent contact with the instructional supervisor and felt no connection to her. Isaac, who never participated in school activities, expressed that his one regret from high school was not joining a basketball team.

Isaac had a mentor for five years who worked with a social service program designed to support youth struggling in school or involved in the juvenile justice system. Once or twice a month Rocco met with Isaac. "Most of our kids are not in school, we hope they get a GED," Rocco looked at Isaac, "He is the only one that might graduate and could go to college." With the exception of helping Isaac register for a charter school in the summer of 2008, Rocco did not really provide academic guidance or support. Isaac called Rocco when he needed something, which generally involved assistance meeting basic needs. Rocco might encourage Isaac to attend school when he dropped off money for a haircut, bus tokens or a winter coat, but they had inconsistent contact.

Future aspirations

Isaac envisioned completing a high school diploma and college degree. His day-to-day activities did not reflect that goal. "I don't really go right now. School don't really fit in, but when I was younger it was better than it is now," Isaac had a matter-of-fact look as he discussed school. His voice lowered when I asked him why he was not actively pursuing his educational goals, "The only reason is because I get to stay home, but when I think about it, I do need to be in school. I don't want to be 20 when I graduate."

He aspired to be a professional basketball player; working for the fire department was his backup. When I asked him to explain the steps necessary to achieve these goals, he shrugged, "I do my work in school and graduate, make sure I don't get distracted by anything bad that can mess me up or not do anything that would get me in trouble where I could go to jail." He paused and took a deep breath, "I just got to try. There is a good chance that I could get distracted, but I am going to try and not let it happen." He smiled as he gave more specific information about what could distract him. "Like girls and stuff. Like a girl could come and I could say that I am going to do my work later and I keep saying I will do it later and it never gets done," he adjusted his oversized shirt, "or going to jail. Just don't do nothing bad outside that could mess me up. I don't do nothing, but I'm just saying." Isaac became less and less hopeful as got closer to his 18th birthday.

At the end of this study Isaac had sophomore-level credits, was not enrolled in school, and did not understand the educational process. He was six months from turning 18. Isaac had no one in his social network guiding him. His residential environment lacked collaboration, which resulted in high levels of conflict, and frequently he abused substances to avoid dealing with the chaos and crowded conditions. Several days a week he came home late at night intoxicated. Two weeks before the end of the study, he was accused of stealing a neighbor's computer. Isaac was questioned by the police, but he denied involvement. The general opinion of his residence supported the neighbor's claim of guilt and rumors began to surface that he was breaking into homes to support his drug and alcohol consumption.

5

JUAN DREAMS BIG

"Tell me about living in the apartment," I inquire.

"Well, it kinda difficult with so many people," Juan shrugs, "sometimes you do things and they don't like it, like when my brother listens to music, my aunt start complaining cause she don't like that kind of music that my brother listens to, so she's complaining about it and all of a sudden my grandpa is complaining because he say we're not organized, like we all be leaving a big mess. So I try my best to keep everything organized and not to bother them."

Juan, who is 5'7" with a thin frame, has large brown eyes and a hint of a mustache. He is a proud Salvadorian American who loves soccer. Juan's curly dark hair is cut short on the sides with a mound on the top and a lock in the back that hangs down to his shoulders—a visual symbol of unity with several other members of the high school soccer team. He has a passive demeanor in front of authority figures, but his friends experience an outgoing side of his personality that includes frequent affirmations and physical acts of affection. Juan does not have many natural gifts, but he compensates for his shortcomings with passion and a strong work ethic. This transfers to all aspects of his life from the classroom to the soccer field. He also uses these skills when pursuing girls.

Juan's residential mobility is more complex than the three other youth and involves family separation and immigration. His grandmother moved from El Salvador to California two years prior to Juan's birth. She worked as a housekeeper in Beverly Hills and saved money to help bring her family members to California. She tried to get Juan's mother to move without legal citizenship before becoming pregnant to ease the documentation process for her future grandchildren. Juan's mother refused. His grandmother studied for and passed the residency test when he was in elementary school. As she accumulated money she sent for family members to join

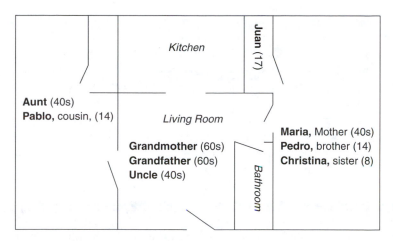

FIGURE 5.1 Juan's apartment

her. "My grandmother was trying to make us come here, and she wanted us to take like a coyote, a person who you give money and they sneak you here," Juan explains, "but she tried to arrange the papers for us and we got residence so we moved here."

Juan lives in a two-bedroom apartment in Echo Park (see Figure 5.1). He shares a room with his mother and two siblings. His aunt and cousin use the other bedroom. The living room is shared by his grandmother, her boyfriend (who Juan calls his grandfather), and his grandfather's son. The living room has a rollaway bed in the corner for his grandparents. The bedroom he shares with his mother and siblings has clothes and toys scattered across the floor. His mother converted the closet into a bedroom for Juan. His bed takes up the majority of the floor space and pictures of professional soccer players, female models and his friends cover the minimal wall space. The shelf at the top of the closet serves as a dresser and storage. His grandfather mounted an additional shelf to the wall at the foot of his bed that he uses to display soccer and academic awards. His brother anxiously awaits Juan's departure for college and has already begun to make plans to move into the closet.

His residential situation made home observations difficult. His aunt gets upset when Juan had visitors at the house. To avoid conflict, Juan ate dinner a few days a week at a friend's house. Halfway through the study he began working most evenings and weekends at a fast food restaurant, which further complicated observations because he rarely spent time at home. I observed places he frequented and used ethnographic interviews to get a sense of his residential situation.

A day in the life of Juan

Morning

Juan's alarm goes off at 7:15. He reaches over, shuts it off before rubbing his eyes and opening the closet door where he sleeps. His mother, Maria, left two hours earlier in order to get to her morning job on time. She works as a housekeeper at a hospital in the morning and a convalescent home in the afternoon. He quietly gets his things together and takes a shower. He returns a few minutes later to wake his siblings. Juan goes into the kitchen to make pancakes while his brother and sister get dressed for school. He takes great care not to make too much noise. His grandfather is asleep in the living room and his aunt and cousin are in the other bedroom. His cousin, who has a physical disability impairing his ability to walk, will be picked up near the entrance to the apartment after Juan has left for school. Yesterday his aunt yelled at Juan because the music coming from his small alarm clock could be heard in the kitchen. He offered to shut the closet door and use a small reading lamp while doing his homework in bed, but she told his grandfather to deal with the issue. His grandfather, who does not like being disturbed, yelled at Juan for being disrespectful. He does not want another argument to ensue this morning. His mind briefly dreams of a day in the future when his family can get their own place.

Pedro and Christina, his younger siblings, sit at the small kitchen table quietly eating their breakfast. Pedro is a stocky ninth grader who dislikes when his brother gives advice or directions. Juan sees a lot of potential in Pedro. School comes easier to Pedro, but he does not exert much effort and prefers hanging out with friends. "Did you get your homework done?" Juan whispers. Pedro mumbles an affirmation. After eating, they clean the kitchen, grab backpacks and quietly walk through the living room and out the door. "Do you have your homework?" Juan asks as he closes the door. His brother and sister nod. This week, Juan is responsible for walking his sister to school, but he calls out a reminder to his brother, "Don't forget I got a soccer practice tonight. You need to pick her up." His brother nods. Juan tells Christina to hurry; he does not want to be more than a few minutes late to school.

After dropping his sister off at school, he turns toward his high school and quickens his pace. The owner of a liquor store sweeping the sidewalk pauses to let him pass. Juan smiles, "Gracias." A block away a young man wearing baggy jeans, an oversized red shirt, red Converse All Stars, and red baseball cap turned to the side is standing on the corner with a few similarly dressed friends. He tried to get one of Juan's friends to join the neighborhood gang a few months ago, but his friend declined and has feared retaliation since. Turning a block early and taking a slightly longer route allows Juan to avoid a confrontation.

Daytime

Juan hears the first period bell ring as he approaches the school's front entrance. His pace accelerates to a near jog. The security guard waves Juan through without looking up from the newspaper he is reading. Juan quietly walks into the orchestra class and finds his saxophone. His teacher does not know the specifics of Juan's situation, but appreciates that many students have circumstances influencing their ability to arrive to school on time. As long as Juan finishes the assignment for today, his teacher will not comment about arriving late. The teacher has everyone play the song that will be graded on Friday. Then he breaks students into small groups to provide feedback while the other students listen. The final few minutes of class are spent cleaning and putting away instruments.

Juan sees a friend from his second period class as he walks out of the orchestra room. Juan pats him on the back, "What's up man?" The two boys comment about a few girls who pass by on their way to class. Juan sits at the back of the classroom with a group of his soccer teammates. His economics teacher has instructions written on the board: "Read pages 112 to 118. Do problems 1–10 and 14 on page 119." The teacher stands as the bell rings and goes over the directions, "Put them in my basket when you are done." The students open their books as the teacher sits down to work on his computer. Juan and his friends help each other find the answers. They finish the assignment with ten minutes remaining and begin talking quietly about preparing for the soccer playoffs. The teacher stands as the bell rings, "Please turn in your assignments." Juan puts his paper in the basket on the way out the door.

He walks with guys from the soccer team to the cafeteria; they have 15 minutes to get breakfast and hang out. He sits next to one of his best friends, Paul. "Hey, you got a date for the Valentine's dance?" Paul asks. "We will see how tomorrow goes," Juan smiles, "I am gonna ask Shorty, but if she says no there is that girl from the party." "You mean the big one?" Paul's eyebrows raise. Juan nods. The bell rings a few minutes later and the boys walk together toward their next classes. Juan pats Paul on the back as they turn down different halls, "See ya later."

Juan says hello to his English teacher as he enters class. The older man nods without looking up from his stack of papers. The majority of students in class are learning English as a second language. The teacher begins by calling students' names as he passes out graded essays. He provides a lot of feedback on the papers, but does not know students by name. He does a short lesson about the major grammatical errors present in the essays and the remainder of class time is spent discussing the novel they are reading.

Juan heads to the college center to do service hours necessary for graduation. As he puts down his backpack, the counselor asks, "Juan, can you take this slip for me?" "Sure," he takes the hall pass and walks to the other side of the school to deliver it to a student he does not know. The two walk back to the counseling office together without talking. He returns to the table where his backpack sits and reads without interruption until the bell rings.

Chemistry is his final and favorite class of the day. Today, in preparation for tomorrow's test, the teacher goes over sample questions while encouraging students to ask questions and take notes. If a student answers correctly, he asks why. If a student is incorrect, he asks the class to help out. "Does anyone have any last minute questions?" he asks before the class ends. The students remain silent. "Alright, I will be here for a while after school if you think of anything." A few students approach his desk as the bell rings. Juan has a question, but soccer practice begins in ten minutes. This is the final week of practice before playoffs; he decides to make an effort to get to class a few minutes early tomorrow in order to ask his question.

He walks out of the locker room with his team in a group. Juan sees his instrument teacher—the basketball coach—walking in the direction of the weight room, "Hey Coach." His teacher looks up, "Hey Juan, congrats on the league championship." Juan smiles, "Thank you." "Good luck this weekend," the coach continues walking. Juan nods, "See ya tomorrow." The varsity soccer team finished the season undefeated and starts the playoffs this weekend. The assistant coach, Antonio, stretches the team out. He was a star player on the team last year and now attends a community college in Los Angeles. "Alright," the head coach yells, "everyone huddle up." The team congregates on and around the benches. "Congrats again on a great season. Now we need to get ready for playoffs," Coach Swain looks at the notes on her clipboard, "I had my meeting with the other coaches yesterday. We get home field for the first round cause we are the top team going into playoffs." The players cheer. "Today we are going to scrimmage against the JV team," she points to the group of boys stretching in the middle of the field. For the next hour, Juan and his team practice. At 4:30, Coach Swain calls them over to the bench. "You all are playing well," she notes, "but you need to make sure we are communicating and working as a team." She provides a few examples before letting them go. Juan walks with Paul into the locker room to get their things. The two boys grab their backpacks and walk home together. Winning the championship consumes their attention.

Evening

Juan comes into the apartment at 5:30. His grandfather, who is sitting on the couch next to the door, looks up from the television. Juan greets him in Spanish as he shuts the door, "Who's winning?" His grandfather explains that his favorite soccer team, Chivas Guadalajara, is losing. "Ah, I told you they were not that good," Juan jokes. His grandfather grimaces, "What do you know?" Pablo sits on the rollaway bed in the corner that his grandfather uses. His aunt, who Juan does not get along with, stirs meat in a pan. He chooses not to say anything. Christina and Pedro are playing in his family's bedroom. "Did you do your homework?" he asks as he places his things in the closet. They shake their heads. "You need to get started." His sister pulls her homework out of her backpack and begins to work on her math assignment. As he heads into the bathroom to take a shower, his brother, who is stretched out on the bed, has not begun to work. "Don't you got work to do?" Juan pauses to ask. His brother shrugs, "I don't know." Juan shakes his head out of frustration; he frequently tries, without success, to motivate his brother.

His mother arrives at 6:15 to the smell of chicken and beans. She walks through the living room without speaking to her father and sister who are eating in front of the television. Her children are scattered around the small bedroom. Juan lays on his bed with the door closed part of the way. Christina looks up from the math worksheet as her mother sits on the bed, "Hola mama." Maria is too tired to do more than smile.

Juan's mother goes into the kitchen to make dinner, but she makes sure not to disrupt the leftovers that her sister has sitting on the stove. The two families do not share food, dishes or storage areas. Maria browns hamburger meat and heats refried beans in a sauce pan. At 6:30 she eats with her children in the kitchen. After dinner, Juan steps into the living room where his aunt, grandfather and Pablo sit watching television. "How was school?" Juan asks his cousin. "What do you care?" Pablo glares at him. As Juan turns towards his bedroom his aunt calls him back, "I don't want hear that radio today. This house is too crowded. You think you run this place." Juan, without responding, goes into the closet to read for his English class. At 9:00, his siblings and mom go to bed. Juan shuts his door and does homework by the small light in the closet until 10:00.

Weekend

Juan wakes up before his alarm. Today playoffs begin. This is his opportunity to become a part of redeeming the school's winning tradition and establish a legacy as a senior. He arrives to locker room two hours before the game. Juan's team enters the first round with high expectations. The assistant coach offers words of encouragement as he leads them through stretches, "Tonight is the first step towards getting back our title." The team cheers. High fives are enthusiastically exchanged. A school bus parks on the street. Juan watches as the rival team, who barely qualified for playoffs, steps off the bus wearing orange uniforms.

Coach Swain calls the team over to the bench. "I am so proud of you guys. You worked real hard this year. And we are league champions," she pauses as the team cheers louder than before. Juan and several of his teammates look over to see if the visiting team can hear what they will be up against. Their competitors do not acknowledge hearing the cheer. "Now we need to stay focused and work as a team," she looks at the assistant coach, "You call out the starting lineup while I go with the captain for the coin flip." Juan hurt his ankle during practice this week and is unsure how long he will be able to play. He remembers how nervous he was to tell his mother about the injury; she does not support his passion for soccer. Several times she has asked him to quit. She fears he may get hurt and the family lacks medical insurance. His mother took him to the emergency room on Wednesday to find out the severity of his injury. "I told you this would happen. That is why I do not want you to play," his mother shook her finger as tears formed in Juan's eyes. She lectured him for two hours as they sat in the waiting room. He tries to put that out of his mind for now. "Juan, you are gonna start, but let me know if it hurts too bad," the assistant coach points to Juan's foot. "Okay coach," he stands and joins the lineup. He scans the bleachers. Fifty students and a handful of parents have come to support the team. His mother, who does not attend today, has never seen him play. Juan sighs and runs to his position on the field.

Each member of the starting lineup finds his place on the field. The cheerleaders wave pompoms above their heads, "Go Bellevue go!" They continue the same cheer throughout the first half of the game. Two minutes into the game the captain of the visiting team makes a fast break. He approaches the goalie, Juan's friend Paul. The move catches the defenders, including Juan, off guard. Paul, who generally has good instincts, blocks left. The ball flies high right. Paul yells at his two defenders out of frustration, "Where were you?" The rival team swarms the captain as Juan pats his friend on the back, "It's okay, we will get them." Throughout the first half both teams have opportunities, but the halftime score favors the visiting team: 1 to 0.

Juan sits on the bench with the other starters. "Don't worry, we're doing fine," Coach Swain shuffles her notes, "We need to make some adjustments. The middle of the field is acting like you don't know what to do. You are letting them control the ball." She pauses as the police helicopter hovering over a nearby neighborhood gets close. She raises her voice, "You need to look at each other and listen. Don't get frustrated, we just need to play our game." The helicopter moves a few blocks away and turns on a spotlight. The assistant coach offers a few words of encouragement, "This is our chance to get the trophy back. It is only a one point game. We have come back before." With a minute remaining before the start of the second half, the entire team forms a circle with one hand in the middle, "Bellevue pride." The crowd cheers.

Juan plays the entire game. Although a slight limp is evident, he tries not to let the pain impact the game. His team nearly scores five times, but the game ends as the first half did. Tears form in Juan's eyes as he gets in line to shake hands with the winning team. The Bellevue team creates a circle in the center of the field around the team captain. He says a few words. Each of the team members puts his right hand in the center. "Bellevue pride," the group murmurs. The apathetic cheer is barely heard over the footsteps of the departing audience. Juan sits next to Paul on the bench. Tears stream down both of their faces. The rival team forms a circle at the center of the field and chants their school name as the shoulders and heads of the Bellevue team slump further down. "Anything can happen in life, and this is one of those things that happens, but they can't take an undefeated season from you," the coach pauses as the team wipes tears dripping from their chins. She tries in vain to make eye contact with each of the young men, "Some of you may come back next year and others of you may play in college, but that is probably the last thing on your mind right now. I am still proud of you, you made a lot of improvements this year." The team does not respond. The assistant coach takes a step forward, "Defense played really well, only one small error. They were playing kickball, which is not the kind of ball we play. You all did well today." The coaches look at each other. "Well, does anyone have anything to say?" Coach Swain looks at the team. Juan uses the end of his jersey to wipe his eyes. No one speaks. "This is probably the last thing you want to do," Coach Swain pulls a screwdriver out of her backpack, "but it is time to take the goals down for the season." The team slowly stands and moves towards the goal posts. As Juan takes the screwdriver,

Coach Swain embraces him, "You did a good job today." He slowly nods his head as she releases her embrace. The team deconstructs both goal posts. Each is placed in a storage bin until next year when another group of varsity players will attempt to redeem Bellevue's reputation.

He slowly limps home with Paul in silence. Tomorrow Juan will begin submitting applications to fast food restaurants. His grandfather lost his job this week and his mother is down to one job. The residence needs another income.

Reflecting on risk and protective factors

Juan was an outgoing high school student who enjoyed playing soccer. Juan used school work and activities as an escape from the conflict within his residence. Unlike Isaac, Juan had lived in the same residence for several years. He intentionally developed relationships that he felt would help him reach his educational goals. Educational success held the promise of future stability and independence.

Residential history and context

His grandmother moved to the United States in the late 1980s and began working as a housekeeper. Juan was born a few years later in El Salvador. After his grand-mother was granted permanent residency and saved money, she sent for her relatives. First Juan's aunt and cousin moved to Los Angeles, then his uncle, and finally Juan's mother and family. His dad was unable to secure the necessary paperwork to join his family because his parents were not married at the time. Initially his father intended to move to California and reunite with his family within a year, but a romantic relationship developed with a woman in El Salvador and complicated his decision. When discussing his father's choice, Juan's voice softened, "Now he has a new girl and don't want to leave." He only spoke to his father once during high school.

Juan moved into the current location with his family and attended the same high school since arriving in the country. "It was hard at the beginning, I did not know English and it was hard to communicate with others. I remember being alone most of the time, but then some friends started talking to me." Over 90% of the students attending Bellevue High School were Latino and most spoke Spanish with varying degrees of fluidity. His limited English abilities created more challenges in class than social settings. Juan enjoyed the social aspects of high school, "With time I started to speak English and I got a lot of friends. And since I got into a soccer team a lot of people in the school know me."

The two-bedroom apartment shared with members of his extended family was a contrast to the three-bedroom home his immediate family had in El Salvador.

> It was really big, I got plenty of room to play with my friends, I invite my friends over and always be around with them, and now right here I don't have the space to do that. It's kinda hard because you lose a lot of things that

you are not allowed to do no more, like do some noises because the neighbors might complain about it, so. Sometimes my little sister runs, she start running around the apartment, the lady downstairs be complaining all the times.

His grandmother made room in the already crowded apartment. His aunt, uncle and cousin had one bedroom; his other aunt and cousin had the other; and Juan's family shared the living room with his grandparents. A year later his uncle moved out after a family argument. His mother had a job by that time and was able to contribute to the bills. Juan's residence split the $900 rent and space evenly between the three households. The physical space within the residence was similarly divided.

The households in Juan's residence collaborated infrequently. Juan's mother and aunt took turns making dinner for his grandfather because his grandmother stayed in Beverly Hills during the week with her employer. However, the two women did not share the kitchen. His aunt would cook between 5:00 and 6:00 in the evening; his mother had the kitchen after 6:00. Two refrigerators stood in the kitchen; one for each woman to use. "It is crazy, my aunt would rather food go bad and throw it away than let us eat it," Juan was frustrated by the lack of collaboration. His mother did not want to live with extended family and Juan frequently encouraged her to find a new apartment. I asked Juan to discuss his view of families choosing to live together for cultural reasons. He reflected:

> That is true, some people. My grandmother, she does. She is trying to keep all the family in a little space, even though she knows it might cause problems, but she likes to do it. I don't really like it, cause it creates a lot of problems and sometimes that is why you don't get along with your own family. My mom would have her own place.

He explained that his family did not move "cause my mom don't have the facilities to move to another place yet." He paused, "She told me as soon as she gets another job, she plans to get two jobs, as soon as she gets it, she plans to move to another place."

Juan's residence had a head of the household. His grandfather served as an authoritarian, but his grandmother was the mediator and decision-maker. However, his grandmother spent the majority each week with her employer. For nearly 20 years she had served as a live-in housekeeper and assistant for a woman in Beverly Hills. Juan felt his grandfather, who was actually his grandmother's boyfriend and not biologically related to him, made decisions in an unfair manner:

> He doesn't seem to care as much about us as my aunt. I think that he doesn't care, our room could be all messy and our room could need to be painted and he won't tell the owner, but if it be my aunt, he would go and tell the landlord immediately.

Conflict occurred frequently. The main points of contention focused on space and resource distribution. The semi-stable environment was frequently threatened by conflicts that were further fueled by the loss of employment. Both his mother and grandfather lost jobs during the study. Since arriving in the United States his mother worked either two or three jobs simultaneously. Two months into the study she was working one part-time job at a nursing home next to Juan's school and his grandfather was unemployed. Financial instability increased the level of conflict and decreased the certainty about their residential future. During the last month of the study, his grandfather's son moved to Los Angeles from El Salvador and slept on the couch in the apartment. The new addition led to further arguments about space and financial responsibilities.

Social network

A social person by nature, Juan met several friends through work and school. He spent the majority of his time outside of his family's apartment. Playing soccer led to the development of relationships with coaches and players, including the head coach, Mrs. Swain, who had no children of her own, but devoted a significant amount of time to her students and players. "I consider her like a grandmother cause she has been there to help me out with most of the things. She tells me to apply to everything to get financial aid and to get into a good college," Juan smiled, "She considers me as a potential kid and a good player and an asset to the team. I really love her."

Juan identified five close friendships. Paul, the goalie on the soccer team, was like a "brother." Paul's family lived in a house that Juan described as "pretty big, bigger than mine. There are not a lot of people there." A few nights each week Paul's mother invited Juan to stay for dinner. Juan enjoyed the peaceful evening dinners. In addition to playing soccer together, they confided in each other about girlfriends, future aspirations and family concerns. When I asked Paul about his plans for college, he looked away, "I am only a junior. I missed a semester, so I am not gonna graduate this year." He took a semester off last year because "things came up, but I was doing okay in school." He returned to school and expected to get an academic athlete award. He had a 3.2 GPA, but was more interested in athletic opportunities. "I am thinking about going pro down in Mexico," The speed of his words increased, "I can punt and throw pretty good, not a lot of people do that." "Yeah," Juan added, "he has a really big leg and can kick better than most people."

Angela was a "good friend" and one of Juan's few female friends that he has not dated. She wanted to go to college, but her status as an undocumented student has made the process difficult. "She is one of my best friends, I know her since two years ago. She has become very important to me, she is like the big sister I never had," Juan paused, "She is pretty smart when she wants, she is an A student, but she is illegal."

Juan and the assistant coach (a community college student who was a former player) worked on Saturday nights stuffing newspapers for the *Los Angeles Times*.

In addition to strengthening their relationship, Juan also befriended three coworkers: Gerardo, Phillipe and Nico. Juan described the three brothers, who also attend school with Juan, as "pretty nice, I usually go to their house before I go to the newspaper, they work in the same newspaper, they are the ones that tell me to keep trying and not to stop, but do my best." They encouraged him to go to college. He quit this job during the last month of data collection, because his family needed extra financial support after his grandfather lost his job. A friend's mother, a fast food restaurant manager, was short staffed and offered to hire Juan. He worked approximately 22 hours each weekend to help his family pay bills and to save money for college expenses. "It is really hard," Juan confessed, "but every successful person needs to struggle first."

Educational factors

Juan attended the same high school all four years and only missed school when he or his sister was sick. "One time I was really sick, I couldn't stand to be in school, my head hurt a lot. The other was that I had to take care of my little sister, we had no one to take care of her." However, he frequently arrived late to school. "Sometimes I wake late, really late. Sometimes because of my sister, I got to take her to school." During the first interview he estimated that he was late to school seven out of the previous ten school days.

Juan was recognized at the end of his junior year for his academic achievement. "I got a medal from my academy. I was highest GPA in my academy, a 4.0. I just kept doing my homework, and when I saw my name on the wall I couldn't believe it." He hoped to earn the same recognition at the end of his senior year. Balancing school, family responsibilities, and work proved to be more difficult than he expected. Juan worked hard to meet the requirements in each class. He only spoke with teachers to address specific questions about assignments. His chemistry teacher was the exception:

> I love chemistry, you learn a lot. Most of the stuff I find really interesting, and my teacher is always trying to help us out, he knows the chemistry is hard, so he is always giving his best and willing to help us out and stay after school, and he goes over the test before we take it. He really does that a lot. He is really willing to talk about anything, even when you got a problem or you need to talk about college or stuff like that, he is always willing to give you information and things like that. Like where the college is at, what requirements you got to meet to get in there, and also he is always bringing information about tutoring programs and stuff like that.

The high school soccer team allowed Juan to develop relationships with an educator and a few academically focused students. His eyes brightened as he spoke about playing on the high school team, "Well, that is what I love to do." The team won the city championship 14 out of the 15 years leading up to his senior year. After losing, Juan was discouraged, "It was kinda sad for us. I don't know, we were being so selfish, we got like team problems. Some of my friends did not get along with the captains and they started a conflict." He was recognized at the athletic banquet for outstanding performance. "My coach said I always put my heart into it, and I play with a lot of intensity and I never give up," he smiled, "even when we are losing like 5–0, I keep on telling them 'Keep running, keep running, keep doing it.'" The soccer team had two coaches: a head coach and an assistant coach who was a player on the team last year. Juan recalled how the assistant coach offered advice about soccer and college:

> He about my age, he was soccer player from Bellevue. I get along with him, I actually work with him. He is in college in Glendale. I talk to him, when we are in school I refer to him as a coach, when we are outside we are just friends. Sometimes I talk to him about what can I do or what am I doing wrong on the field and he try to help me out to teach me how to do things right. And then I talk to him outside about college, is it hard there and things like that. He says it is really hard, it is not like high school no more. He told me he graduated from Bellevue with a 3.7 GPA, and actually he is getting Ds in college.

When I asked if the assistant coach spoke with him about the difference between college and high school, Juan nodded. "Yeah, the teachers are not on your case no more. It is all yourself. He is right," Juan paused, "the teachers are no longer after your case, it is not their problem if you do your work or not, and you are paying for a class. If you do not pass it you got to pay again and repeat it again."

Juan signed up for a college mentoring program during his senior year. He met with his mentor, a university professor, two or three times a month to discuss the college application process. During the first interview, Juan gave an example of their conversations, "Like right now we are working on the financial aid ID, we go over what I need to do, he tell me what I need to bring, like my social security number, and then we go over it." His mentor provided advice and guidance. "He always check about how I am doing and ask what is going on in my life," Juan explained. "I try to tell him the truth. Cause I know he is a really good person and he can give me advice about what to do and what not to do." Juan's mentor agreed to continue working with him while attending college.

Future aspirations

Juan's initial response when I asked him about school was similar to the other youth. In a matter-of-fact tone, he explained, "I spend most of my time in school. Actually, I spent like 8 or 12 hours doing school work." Unlike Isaac, he also viewed education as an opportunity to avoid negative behaviors and secure a stable future. School, for Juan, was a way to escape the potentially detrimental influences of his neighborhood:

> it keep me away from gangs and things like that and actually I like to study because I want to become a doctor. I know that if I want to do that I need to go to school and do a lot of things, so it keeps me apart from doing bad things.

He got frustrated that teachers did not always provide rigor or support he felt was necessary to adequately prepare him for college. For example, he shared an experience about his first year in high school, "My English teacher didn't care about me, he was like 'if you don't know, you got to learn.' And I was always going to him for help and he didn't do anything for me."

Education was also an avenue to help his community. He planned to eventually return to his community after graduating college. "I want to be a doctor cause I saw a lot of people dying before my eyes [in El Salvador] and I just want to help my community," Juan shared during our second interview, "I want to help others. The earthquake in El Salvador, back in 2001, there was an earthquake and my community collapsed and I saw a lot of people die. A lot of people were sick and miserable, and I just felt like I wanted to help." "Do you want to go back to El Salvador?" I inquired. Juan shrugged his shoulders, "I want to be a doctor wherever as long as I help others."

Both Isaac and Juan lived in "separate households" that were plagued by conflict. However, their participation in the 2008–09 school year differed dramatically. Juan applied to and was accepted to eight universities. Initially, he planned to enroll at the University of California in Riverside because he felt his chances of playing soccer at the collegiate level would be better there than a Division I school. After speaking with his college mentor, he decided to attend the University of California in Los Angeles. Financial aid was his biggest concern. Scholarships, grants and personal savings only covered about 60% of college costs. He planned to attend a summer bridge program that focused on the transition to college and improving writing skills. Juan saved money from his job to pay for the housing deposit and planned to live on campus all four years of college. I attended a campus visit with him during the spring. As we walked to the car after the tour, Juan smiled, "I really picture myself coming here and doing well."

PART II
Merged Residences

Merged residences involved homes where individuals and families "merged" into a single unit. This arrangement had a positive influence on the youth's educational participation. Living in a merged residence did not guarantee success in high school, but it served as a protective factor. The residential structure and social network of each participant worked together to shape educational resilience. I share the experiences of two youth living in merged residences—Kylee and Marco. The chapters in this section are similarly structured, including background information, a day in their lives, and analysis of risk and protective factors.

6

KYLEE GOES WITH THE FLOW

"Tell me what you do after school," I ask during the first interview.

"Well, I don't have homework because I don't like to come home and do homework cause I'm like the only," Kylee pauses, "well, my mom doesn't know what I do in school, like she doesn't get it, I can't ask nobody younger than me, so I do it at school and then when I come home it's just sit around a lot."

Black-rimmed glasses with a missing arm perch lopsided on Kylee's nose like opera spectacles. She stands 5'7" with a round face. She prefers to identify as "American" and does not necessarily embrace her Mexican American heritage. Although shy when unfamiliar with her surroundings, Kylee has a loud personality and enjoys being funny. After school hours she trades her white polo for a tight-fitting T-shirt that accentuates her well-fed physique. Isaac and Kylee live in dramatically different residential contexts, but they share a limited understanding of the educational process. Both aspire to attend college. Neither has taken steps necessary to reach that goal.

Kylee lost residential stability after the divorce of her parents. Before her parents separated, the family lived in a lower-middle-class neighborhood. Kylee proudly announces that her dad's side of the family "has money," but a rift between her mother and his family has negatively impacted her relationship with them. Her father infrequently calls to check on them.

Kylee moved with her mother to several different places before the current location. Her mother, Lucy, and a friend, Angela, agreed to share household, financial and childrearing responsibilities. Lucy collects welfare benefits while attending a job training program and Angela works two fulltime jobs. Kylee currently lives in a three-bedroom apartment in Watts (see Figure 6.1). Each of the mothers has a bedroom and their children share the third room. The living room, 8' by 15' with maroon carpet, has

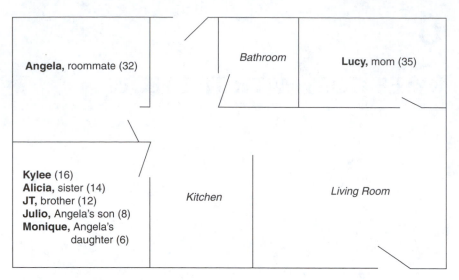

FIGURE 6.1 Kylee's apartment

two forest-green couches that are frequently rearranged. A 40" flat-screen television sits on a small stand. Next to each couch is a small end table. No pictures hang on the white walls. Toys and food are strictly prohibited from the living room. The kitchen has a small, round table in the corner with one bench. The oven has not worked for nine months; the family cooks all meals on the stove top. A dish rack sits next to the sink, but dishes are washed and placed back in the cupboards after each use. The diligent cleaning and organizing makes the cozy apartment feel spacious.

Her mother's bedroom, a 10' by 12' room with a double bed and small dresser, is at times used by all of her children. The door remains shut, but when opened the smell of marijuana fills the living room. Angela, the mother of the other family, leaves her door open unless she is sleeping. Her room has a double bed with a homemade quilt. Two dressers line one of the walls. The top of each dresser is covered with small pictures and personal items.

I spent a few hours each Tuesday night with the family. As our relationship developed I was invited to participate in additional activities, including a baptism and birthday party. During the first month of the study, I felt the family was more comfortable when I scheduled visits. Their comfort level increased as our relationship evolved and then I was invited to stop by the home unannounced.

A day in the life of Kylee

Morning

The alarm goes off at 5:00. Kylee, 16 years old, hits the snooze button and drifts back to sleep for nine more minutes. She shares a bedroom with her two siblings and two other children. A set of bunk beds lines one wall of the 8' by 10' room. The wall perpendicular has another set of bunk beds. The room is crowded, but not messy. Each child has a plastic bin with two drawers for their clothes. Bins of the younger children are on the floor; those of the teenagers are stacked on top.

The second alarm pulls her out of bed. She needs to get in the shower before everyone wakes up. Kylee picks up her school uniform, laid out the night before, and heads to the bathroom. She likes having time to herself in the morning; she does not need to speak to anyone until she is fully awake. After showering, she flat irons her long hair before pulling it back in a ponytail. Kylee comes back in the room yelling, "Rise and shine!" The younger children roll over and shield their eyes from the light. Alicia, her 14-year-old sister, hates that her sister turns on the light without warning. She gives Kylee a dirty look as she slowly walks toward the bathroom. "I hate you," Alicia grumbles. "Whatever," Kylee laughs, "you know you love me." Kylee stands in front of the mirror, frustrated by the lack of individuality she can exhibit. The white polo and blue pants restrict her sense of style and self-expression. She makes a few minor adjustments. A pink barrette holding back her bangs completes her look. Alicia, who has a similar build to Kylee, comes back into the room at 6:10. Alicia appreciates the convenience of a school uniform. Both girls tell the three younger ones to get out of bed and get ready for school.

Kylee heads to the living room as the two boys roll out of bed. She sits on the couch and turns on the morning news. Monique, the roommate's 6-year-old daughter, comes out of the room with her pajamas on and sits next to Kylee. Monique has a mild cognitive impairment and wears a diaper each night to prevent wetting her bed. "You need to get ready for school," Kylee points toward the bathroom. Monique's smile fades as she slumps to the bathroom. Monique is the only other person to shower in the morning; the two boys and Alicia shower before bed. Kylee goes into the kitchen. She pours cereal into a butter container that now serves as a bowl and puts a piece of toast on a napkin. She calls out a time update, "It is 6:30." JT, Kylee's 12-year-old brother, comes out of the room, pauses from rubbing his eyes, and glares at Kylee. She smiles. Monique comes out of the shower and her 8-year-old brother, Julio, helps her get dressed. A few minutes later, Alicia is sitting on the kitchen bench next to Kylee; Julio eats cereal at the kitchen sink. Lucy, Kylee's mother, comes out of her room in pajama pants and a large sweatshirt, "Hurry up you guys." Lucy can have an abrasive tone and expects the children to obey her. Although crass at times, her children see past her tough exterior and feel loved.

Julio and Monique's mother, Angela, arrives home wearing a blue housecleaning uniform. Angela works two jobs. Typically she leaves for her first job at a fast food restaurant before the children get home from school and then heads directly to her night shift cleaning offices at a military base. She says hello to each person as she walks to her room. Her two children follow. This will be their only chance to visit today.

At 7:00 Kylee calls out the final warning. All of the kids have eaten and Alicia washes the dishes. Lucy tells the kids to get their backpacks ready, "And you better make sure the house is clean before we leave." Monique kisses her mom goodbye; Julio's shoulders drop as Angela gives him a hug. He wishes he had more time to spend with his mom. Julio goes back into the bedroom to make his bed. Julio peeks his head out the bedroom door and yells, "Hey, JT didn't make his bed." JT drops his backpack and heads into the bedroom, bumping into Julio in the process. "Hey," Julio frowns, "don't do that." "Boys, knock it off," Lucy commands as she inspects the house in preparation for departure, "Whose shirt is this on the floor?" JT sighs and puts his shirt in the laundry hamper. Lucy approves and waves towards the door, "Alright, everyone get in the fucking car."

At 7:20 all five kids are in the blue 1998 Honda Accord. Since they are running late, Lucy drops off Kylee at the high school first. Then she drives half a mile to drop off JT and Alicia at the middle school, and finally stops by the elementary school where Monique and Julio attend. Lucy returns home at 7:45. It is time for her to eat breakfast and get ready for the day. She needs to finish her homework before driving to the community college to participate in classes through a welfare-to-work grant. She will make the similar tour of schools this evening after their kids finish the afterschool programs—except for Kylee, who gets to walk home on her own.

Daytime

Arriving to school with only a few minutes to spare, Kylee joins the herd of students filing to class. She hates arriving to school late because she feels like everyone in class stares at her. In her first class, medical professions, students work in small groups discussing the ethics of medicine. One of the boys in Kylee's group tells a joke and the group bursts into laughter. The noise catches the teacher's attention. "You need to get back to work," the teacher's thick Indian accent makes it difficult for students to understand the specific words, but the message is clear. Kylee and one of the boys try to redirect the group, but the conversation diverts to a party the previous weekend. A few minutes before class ends they rush to answer the five questions on the worksheet. As Kylee leaves she cannot recall the lesson's purpose, but she is satisfied that she will get full credit for the in-class activity.

She sees Tommy, her current love interest, on the way to media class. He nods in her direction and Kylee turns red. She wishes there was time to talk, but her slow cadence requires continuing in the direction of class or she will be late— she hates running even more than being late. Kylee sits down at her desk as the bell rings. Her media teacher, a man in his sixties with an abrasive demeanor, assigns students a project every two weeks that requires conducting an interview and writing a brief paper structured like an article in a newspaper. The current assignment involves identifying a student who plays a sport. Students have drafted interview questions and today's activity involves practicing the interview with someone in class. Kylee pairs up with the boy sitting next to her. She is unsure who to recruit for the official interview, but looks forward to meeting a new person. The teacher makes a lap around the classroom in an attempt to keep order and ensure that students have begun the assignment. The majority of the time he spends at his desk and occasionally barks out an order, "It's too loud, stay focused."

Class ends and Kylee gathers her things. She sees Yessy in the hall, "Hey shorty." Yessy, who hopes to stand 5'1" before she finishes growing, looks through the bangs covering the left side of her face and smiles. The two girls walk in the same direction to class as Kylee retells how she saw Tommy, "I think he smiled when we passed each other, or maybe I was the one smiling." They both laugh. At the next hallway the girls part ways. Kylee dislikes chemistry, but she does what is necessary to pass. Today's lecture covers the effects of mixing two different types of liquids. Kylee alternates between taking notes and daydreaming about having lunch with her friends. With 20 minutes left in class the teacher passes out a homework assignment designed to test students' knowledge before allowing them access to chemicals. "Next week we will be working in lab," the teacher announces, "Be sure to have all of your homework completed so you can participate." Kylee works with a girl sitting next to her. Before the bell for lunch rings she has finished her homework and packed her things.

Kylee and Katherine stand in line waiting for their lunch before joining friends in the cafeteria. Kylee has a group of ten friends who share a table for lunch, but she primarily speaks to Katherine and Salvador. The conversations range from what has happened in school to recent parties and drama associated with dating. Each person in the group has a role. Yessy is sarcastic; Katherine is quiet. Kylee provides the comedy. "A Black man and a Mexican are in a car. Who is driving?" Kylee asks the small group of Latinos sitting near her. They all shrug their shoulders and wait for a response. After a short pause she smirks, "The police." The others at the table laugh and share their own related jokes. The entertainment gets interrupted by the school bell. Kylee dumps her trash before shuffling off to class.

The final class of the day is algebra. Kylee vigorously takes notes as the teacher plots algebraic formulas on a line. Kylee understands little of what is being said; she has struggled in math since elementary school. As the lecture drags on she becomes tired and fights the urge to dose off. The teacher asks if students have any questions. The class responds with silence. Kylee would ask a question, but feels so lost that she is unsure what to ask. "Looks like everyone's ready for the homework," the teacher says with a knowing smile. He writes a single problem on the board. He puts the dry erase marker down and turns toward the class, "There you go. You have the remaining class time to start working on your homework." Fifteen minutes remain. Kylee spends this time trying to figure out where to begin. She worries that she will fail the class because she rarely turns in the homework and struggles to pass each exam. The teacher walks around the room and hands each student a midcourse grade. Kylee nervously peeks. She is surprised that she earned a C. Maybe she will pass the class after all. The bell rings. She puts her spiral notebook in her backpack where it will remain until class tomorrow.

She looks for Yessy and Katherine near the school's front entrance. "Hey you two," Kylee smiles, "I think I might be passing all my classes." "Nice," Yessy nods, "I am not sure I am doing too good." The conversation shifts to their current love interests and a party coming up next weekend as they walk home together. When they get to the government housing project on Success Avenue, Katherine says goodbye and heads to her apartment. Kylee and Yessy walk one more block to Yessy's house. Kylee says goodbye and heads home. Her neighbor rides by on a bike holding a plastic bag with three cans of beer. He smiles at her. "Hello," she waves to him and continues her slow pace around the corner to her house.

Evening

Kylee arrives home at 3:30. The house is quiet. Her mother has left to run errands before picking up the other children from their afterschool programs. She drops her backpack on the couch before heading into the bedroom. She cannot wait to take off her school uniform. She picks a pair of blue jeans and a sleeveless shirt that announces: "I ♥ my boyfriend."

Kylee sits on the couch and flips through the television channels until she finds a rerun of *America's Funniest Home Videos*. This is her "me time" before the house gets back in motion; alone time in the apartment is scarce and sacred. An hour later the door opens. "Leave me alone," Alicia yells as she heads to the bedroom. JT laughs. A few minutes later Lucy comes in with Julio and Monique. "Hey, clean your shit up," Lucy orders, "you ain't supposed to just drop your crap in the living room." The kids move backpacks and papers to the bedroom.

Lucy heads into her bedroom. JT and Julio race outside to see who will get on the bike first. Monique follows them, but stops at the door and looks back at Kylee. "Okay," Kylee stands, "let me get my shoes." She escorts Monique outside as the smell of marijuana begins to seep into the living room. JT and Julio argue about who gets to ride the blue miniature mountain bike first. Both boys pull on the handlebars. Two women who live a few houses down the block walk in their direction. "Hey, move out the way," Kylee waves at the boys. Julio moves away from the bike to allow the women to pass. JT jumps on the bike and rides off. Julio sits on the step next to Kylee; he sulks while awaiting his turn. Alicia, taking this opportunity to enjoy some quiet time of her own, stretches out on her bed and listens to the radio.

The brakes of the bike screech as JT abruptly stops in front of the steps. He drops the bike next to Julio and goes to the neighbor's house to play video games as the sun begins to set. Kylee watches as Julio jumps on the bike and heads 20 feet down the block before turning around; he is only allowed to ride within eyesight of the apartment. "Look at me," Monique yells. She has climbed on the hood of Lucy's car and is now making a snow angel in the dust. "What are you doing?" Kylee laughs, "Get off the car and come over here." Monique slides off the hood, slowly walks over to Kylee and sits on the step.

"Dinner," Lucy yells from the kitchen. Kylee inhales deeply as she walks inside with Monique and Julio, "It smells good in here." Lucy has placed potato salad and barbecue beans on the table and now fries chicken wings on the stove. Kylee and Monique share a bench at the kitchen table and start eating. Alicia comes out of the bedroom with her report card, "Look, I passed all of my classes." Her mother reviews the midcourse grades: two As, two Bs and two Cs. "Good job," Lucy nods. Alicia smiles and puts the report card on the refrigerator door. Kylee puts down her fork, "Yeah, I ended up getting a C in algebra." Lucy turns in her direction with dilated pupils and a look of shock, "No fucking way." "I know, that's what I was thinking," Kylee's eyes widen with surprise as she places her plate in the sink and sits on the couch. Julio comes into the kitchen and washes the fork she used; they currently only have two forks. He sits on the bench next to Monique; Alicia joins a few minutes later. JT arrives as they begin to eat and stands at the table. No seats or forks remain, but JT does not mind standing or eating with his fingers.

The three older kids finish eating before heading into the living room. Lucy sits next to Monique who has finished eating the chicken, but now makes designs out of the side dishes. "You need to eat that food right now. Stop playing," Lucy points to the food. Monique continues circling her spoon through the beans. "Eat now," Lucy demands, "or you're going to bed." Monique has made little progress by the time Lucy finishes her meal. "Okay, go to bed. Put a diaper on and get in bed if you don't want to eat," Lucy points toward the bedroom. Monique gets up from the table and slowly walks into the bedroom with her head down. Lucy refuses to waste food; she scrapes Monique's leftovers onto her plate. After finishing dinner she places both plates in the sink.

Lucy joins the children in the living room. Alicia sporadically works on her history homework when *American Idol* goes to commercial break. Lucy sits on the couch next to her and begins making flowers out of tissue paper and dental floss. She volunteered to help coordinate a party for Monique's birthday and baptism. "Here, I want to help," Kylee offers. She twists the paper together and Lucy ties the floss around the bottom. Lucy notices that one flower is wet, "What the fuck are you doing?" Kylee looks up and laughs, "I have to lick my fingers to separate the paper." "You are ruining them," Lucy smiles, "Don't fuckin' lick them any-more." Alicia jumps in, "Yeah, or they will start sticking together like used toilet paper." Everyone laughs. "Yeah, after we finish with the party we can just sit this box next to the toilet," Kylee adds as she adjusts her lopsided glasses. They continue to joke about using the dental floss while on the toilet.

JT interrupts the conversation to ask if he can take a shower. "It is not your day," Lucy responds. JT insists. "Fine, but you ain't gonna take another shower until Saturday." JT comes back from the shower ten minutes later with beads of water dripping from his short hair. "Did you dry off," Kylee asks, "or just shake like a dog?" JT looks at her, "Huh?" Lucy laughs, "That's my boy, shake it like a dog." JT looks confused as Kylee starts laughing. They watch the preliminary rounds of singers and comment on how good or bad they sound. At 8:30 Lucy puts the flowers in the box and shuts off the television, "It is time for chores." JT goes in the bathroom, Alicia and Julio head to the kitchen, and Kylee cleans the living room. The chores take 15 to 20 minutes. The kids organize their uniforms and school supplies for tomorrow. By 9:15 the house is quiet, except for the television. Lucy watches a few shows while talking to a friend on the phone.

Weekend

Kylee has loose plans for the weekend. Saturdays generally start slow. Around 1:00 she walks over to Yessy's house and knocks on the door. The door swings open as Yessy's two young nieces run out. "Get back in the house," Yessy's 20-year-old brother yells. Kylee had a crush on him last fall, but now she finds him annoying. However, she does not mind looking at his muscular, tattooed arms. He notices Kylee's admiration, "What do you want?" Yessy pushes past her brother, "Shut up." The two girls walk down the sidewalk as he herds the kids back into the apartment, "Hey, where are you two going?" Yessy ignores her brother and rolls her eyes. "He such a dumb ass," Yessy laughs as she makes two fists and holds them together in front of Kylee, "but I guess not everyone thinks so." Written in purple marker on her knuckles is the word "C-R-U-S-H-I-N-G." For the past few days she held up her fists whenever her friends saw someone they had a crush on. Kylee shakes her head, "You are crazy." Yessy laughs harder.

They walk through the gate that surrounds the housing project where Katherine lives—this is one of the largest projects in Los Angeles County. Kylee knocks on her door. "Hey." Kylee and Yessy look around but are unsure where the voice came from. "Up here," the voice yells. Katherine's 19-year-old sister is hanging out of the second-floor window and laughing, "We will be right down." A few minutes later Katherine and her sister join them on the front step. Each of the units has a 2' by 3' cement step by the door. A clothes line extends from each apartment to the middle of the lawn where a sidewalk divides the front yard of each unit. Katherine, who has deep-set eyes and slumped shoulders, wears tight blue jeans and a black sweatshirt with Jack's face from *The Nightmare before Christmas*.

"So," Kylee puts her hands on her hips and strikes a model pose, "do you notice anything different?" Her friends look at her for a minute. Kylee's smile fades. She points at her glasses with an exaggerated gesture. "Oh, I thought something was different," Yessy offers. Kylee pushes her new glasses up on her nose, "They are a bit loose, but I didn't want them to take them back. So I said they were fine." Her friends nod and the conversation reaches a pause. "Remember last weekend," Yessy laughs and the girls all look at Katherine's sister. Kylee rolls her eyes, "That was not funny. I be scared. I really wanted to write a will in case we didn't make it back." The girls had gotten bored at Katherine's house and decided to sneak out at 2 o'clock in the morning. They walked a few miles away. "You be having fun when we saw those guys," Katherine covers her mouth as she laughs. "Yeah, well you know me. I yell at every guy I see," Kylee pauses, "well, except for the ones I like.

Then I get nervous." The girls recount how they got tired of walking and stopped in a restaurant to buy coffee. Kylee started dancing around and being silly in front of the other customers. Katherine's sister puts her hand up, "But that was not funny when I laughed too hard and puked coffee out my nose." "Yeah," Kylee frowns, "well, it wasn't cool that I had to go in the bathroom and watch you puke neither."

Kylee notices Tommy walking with a friend on the path between two buildings. "Kylee is crushing," Yessy whispers. Kylee grimaces but does not take her eyes off Tommy. "Hey, what you guys doing?" Katherine's yell catches Kylee off guard. The two boys pause and look in their direction. Tommy, who is thin with curly black hair, struts over to the girls followed by his friend. "What's up?" he stands a few feet away wearing a purple shirt and bulky skateboard shoes. Yessy slowly raises her fists and points them in Kylee's direction. "Not cool," Kylee's eyes glare as she starts to blush. The two boys act as though they do not see the word written in purple ink. "We're gonna go play soccer," Tommy points in the direction they were walking, "We could use some cheerleaders." Kylee's face softens. "Alright, we be right over," Katherine interjects. The two boys walk away and Kylee returns her attention to Yessy, "Not cool." "They didn't know, I could have meant Katherine," Yessy puts her hands in her pocket and grins sheepishly.

The four girls walk around the building. Tommy and five other boys, ranging in age from 7 to 18, organize the field and select teams. The grassy area that serves as the playing area is the space between the two backsides of the apartment buildings. A hat represents one goal post and three boys, including Tommy, take off their shirts to use as the other posts. Kylee's attention focuses on Tommy, who now wears jeans and a white tank top. She takes a deep breath, "I hope that he trips and falls and tears that shirt off." Yessy and Katherine laugh.

After playing for 20 minutes the ball is kicked over the goalie's head and lands near a group of elementary-aged boys. The older boys look in their direction. Everyone pauses. One of the boys reaches down, picks up the ball, and takes off running followed by the group of younger boys. "Ah shit," Tommy's friend, Carlos, sighs before sprinting after them. The kids make it to the other side of the housing project, nearly a mile away, before he catches them. Tommy and the other boys take this opportunity to rest while waiting for the ball to return. They sprawl on the lawn near the girls and chat with each other about the game. The girls whisper and giggle. Neither group acknowledges the other. Carlos returns with the ball ten minutes later. Beads of sweat appear on his forehead as he gasps for breath, "Those little fuckers wouldn't give it back to me." The younger boys peek around the corner of the building. He motions in their direction and they run away laughing.

At 6:00 the sun begins to set. "It's cold, I'm going in," Katherine points toward her apartment. "Hey," Kylee interrupts, "can I check my MySpace?" The girls slowly walk to the apartment and take turns logging on their web pages. The girls spend the next several hours looking at their friends' accounts, changing background designs, and sending messages. "I better go," Kylee begrudgingly confesses, "I gotta be home by 10:00." Yessy and Kylee walk home a few minutes before 10:00.

Reflecting on risk and protective factors

Kylee was a social teenager who enjoyed joking around with friends and family. She strove for uniqueness while not drawing the attention of teachers or administrators. She attended school regularly throughout the study. However, like Isaac, she did not understand the educational process or what steps would need to be taken in order to achieve her goals. Protective factors encouraged her to participate in school; risk factors limited her engagement and may negatively influence her ability to achieve her goals.

Residential history and context

Kylee lived in a three-bedroom apartment in Temecula with her mother and father when she was a toddler. She shared a room with her sister, her brother had his own room, and her parents slept in the remaining room. "There was two bathrooms so it was pretty big for us," Kylee explained. The separation of her parents after nine years of marriage led her mother to seek the support of family and friends. Soon after her parents' divorce, Kylee moved with her mother and siblings into her grandmother's house. She described their first shared residence, "Sometimes it was us and sometimes it was my uncle, and then sometimes it was like another family member from my godmother's side, and then another time it was my aunt and her boy." Kylee's family moved out of her grandmother's house after conflict arose between family members. Her mother, Lucy, spoke with a friend who was willing to split the cost of an apartment. Her three children shared one room and the roommate used the other bedroom. Lucy, who slept in the living room, asked a guy she was dating to construct a wall to divide her space from the living area. Kylee provided a justification for the construction:

> We had to because we had two bedrooms and it was kinda small and then plus we had another roommate so we had to make another bedroom, so we made a bedroom out of the living room, so it was me, my brother and sister in one room, and then the roommate in another room, and then my mom stayed in the living room.

The owner, who was not persuaded by Lucy's justification for the construction, sent an eviction notice via certified mail. Once again the family had no place to stay. They moved into a friend's house for a month. "We didn't have a place, we were...." Kylee's voice trailed off. She looked at the residential timeline we were creating, "There has been a lot of moving and evictions." After a moment she explained that the next residence was a house where they lived for a year, "We got kicked out of that one because we supposedly were being blamed for things breaking and stuff like that, and then we had a dog and they didn't allow that." The family moved to a studio apartment in Colton where a friend had six months remaining on the lease, but wanted to move. "We lived in a studio so there wasn't no bedrooms or anything," Kylee looked at the paper, "It was just me, Alicia, JT, and my mom. Well, because the studio wasn't ours, so when that lease was done we had to move out."

The family moved into the current location nine months before the study began. The $1,200 rent was more than Lucy could afford on a welfare stipend. Kylee explained how her family started living doubled-up for the first time with someone who was not a member of her extended family:

> We knew Angela ever since Temecula, when Alicia was born. And we always kept in touch. My mom was kinda struggling and my mom didn't know where to go. So when she heard about Angela wanting to move out from where she lived, my mom saw it as an opportunity, so my mom was like, "Well, we'll just move with her."

The contributions to the residence were more broadly considered in Kylee's situation than the other residences. "Angela puts her money into the house and I provide the childcare," Lucy shared. Lucy contributed $300 and her roommate paid the remaining $900 as well as the majority of the bills. Lucy's management of household responsibilities (i.e. childcare, cleaning and cooking) compensated for the lower financial contribution. The two households distributed space evenly and the mothers purchased a new car together six months before the study began. "I get a place to live and she don't worry about her kids," Lucy smiled and nodded, "It works out good."

Conflicts arose on occasion within the residence. Lucy took the responsibility for resolving arguments between the children and Angela supported those disciplinary decisions. "I have to be strict right in front of [Angela] so her kids know what's up," Lucy shared when I asked about the kids' behavior. Major disputes between the two mothers occurred rarely and were resolved quickly. The most frequent disagreements between the women were instigated by Angela's family. "I smoke, and I smoke pot, and everybody knew that before we moved in, but now they are getting all bent out of shape," Lucy rolled her eyes. She believed that Angela was not concerned about her drug use, "But she gets around her family and they start listing how the bills get paid and she gets all worked up."

Day-to-day misunderstandings between the women did occur as a result of personality differences. Lucy took words literally and easily got her feelings hurt; Angela was direct and sarcastic. "At first it was hard," Lucy had a serious look, "I would take it to heart when she would say something, but now I am used to it." Angela served as the decision-maker if an issue needed to be resolved. Lucy described the process of conflict resolution:

> Angela will come home sometimes and put me in my place. I will listen and most of the time she is right. She will let things go for a bit, but then she pulls me aside and says something. And she is right. I know that. I apologize.

When I asked her to describe the relationship she has with Angela, Lucy paused, "Well, she is the man of the family."

Although residents managed conflict and merged the two households, there was some uncertainty about the stability of the living arrangement. During the first interview Kylee was frustrated that her mother had mentioned the possibility of moving. Lucy did not feel safe in the neighborhood and wanted to move back to a suburban environment. When I asked if the two families would stay together, she brushed her bangs to the side, "I hope so." Angela and Lucy spoke about the possibility of finding an apartment in a more suburban area. In February Kylee recalled a conversation with her mother about moving:

> I felt kinda bad cause I feel like I am doing real good here now, like my grades are going up and everything, and I like the people here, and it is kinda sad that I am just going to be moving again, and that I am going to have to restart all over again, and stuff. My mom was telling me that we might, I don't know if we are, but we might wait until after I graduate high school to move.

Kylee's residence exhibited the most collaboration of all the residences. Both mothers benefited from the relationship—Lucy received financial support and Angela received childcare. The two women negotiated a relationship that enabled both to have a larger apartment, a new car and childcare.

Social network

Kylee was an outgoing person, but the neighborhood made her nervous. Kylee spent the majority of her time away from school in the apartment or with her two best friends, Katherine and Yessy. Weekday evenings were generally spent in the apartment with her mother, siblings and Angela's two children. Her extended family did not play a major role in her life. The separation of her parents resulted in limited contact with her father or his side of the family.

Her mother, who enrolled in a "Welfare to Work" program a few months after moving to the current residence, received a grant to cover classes and expenses at a community college. Lucy struggled in her remedial English and math classes. One essay she wrote, entitled "My Ideal Roommate," required significant revisions before the instructor would provide a grade. The main argument of her three-paragraph essay was that respect was an important element of successful roommate households. Specifically, she discussed the importance of teaching children to be respectful and not disrupt the roommate's things. As a supporting point she added, "it makes you think twice before having snot noised kids." The entire essay lacked structure and each sentence had grammatical and spelling errors. Her instructor had written a note at the bottom of her first draft: "do not use contractions in academic writing." She read the comment aloud while sitting on the couch watching television with her children. "What the fuck's a contraction?" her glazed eyes looked in Kylee's direction. Kylee just shook her head and laughed. Lucy failed the class after arriving to the final without a blue book. The instructor told her to purchase one and return. "I just fucking left. I was so pissed," she sighed and then explained how she spent the rest of the afternoon in her bedroom. She later found out that she failed both classes. A month before the study ended she was informed that she may be dropped from the educational program. "Oh well," she shrugged, "at least I can say I tried."

Kylee's close friends did not have academic ambitions. Her two best friends attended school because they were required to do so. Graduation from high school was expected to happen, but the three girls did not take steps to ensure success. Postsecondary education was not part of their discourse. Kylee described Yessy, also in 11th grade, as "more like the 'eh, school, forget school' type." Katherine was 18, but struggled to earn sophomore-level credits. Kylee respected her desire to stay in school, but did not think Katherine would make it to graduation. "She's trying, but she's bad [at school]," Kylee shook her head, "like worse than me, I think."

Her friends generally viewed school as a requirement, but few had educational aspirations. Although her friends experimented with drugs and alcohol, they were not regular users. Kylee explained, "Everyone drinks, but not like every Saturday they are going to drink, it is like a once in a while type of thing." When I asked about her substance use, she paused and smiled, "I don't do it, but if they offer it I go ahead and do it. It is rare though, like once in a year rare." After the interview she clarified, "You know I meant drinking stuff not smoking, right. I am afraid of cancer. None of my friends are into drugs."

Kylee could not identify any mentors in her life who provided guidance through school. Her mother expected attendance, but did not understand the educational process.

Educational factors

Kylee attended a comprehensive high school approximately a mile from her home. For as long as she can remember she enrolled in a different school each year. Similar to Isaac, Kylee was highly mobile and had a difficult time remembering all of the transitions:

> At my friends' [house] for a month I didn't go to school that time. I just didn't go, I think it was summer time. No, it wasn't, I just didn't go to school. The last Rialto place, I only had five months of middle school so I went to another middle school and then it was summer break after that and then Colton, I went to one school…no, I went…I'm confused, wait…in the last Rialto, I went to middle school and then I went to a high school. That's when I went to Rialto High, and then I didn't want to be there anymore because the school was really far and I didn't want to be in school anymore so I started home school. And then when I got tired of home I went to a high school by my grandma's house, um, I moved with my grandma and then,

um, after that I didn't really want to stay at my grandma's anymore, so I went back home and that is when we moved and that is when we went to Colton. I was in 10th grade and so I stayed at one school and now I am at another school here. It was a lot.

She remembered eight elementary schools, two middle schools and three high schools. Since settling into the residence, Lucy and Angela set a clear expectation that the children attend school regularly. Kylee was rarely absent.

Kylee attempted to "fly under the radar" at school by avoiding drawing the attention of teachers. Her relationships with her teachers were confined to the classroom context. "If I see all my teachers, I say 'hi,' but that's it, or I ask them what are we doing today or whatever, but it's not outside of school." Her primary goals included passing her classes and not getting in trouble. For example, when I asked to describe her first period teacher she responded:

I don't have problems with him so he is cool. If I'm doing good then you're a cool teacher. You don't have to yell at me, you don't have to do nothing at me, you just tell me I'm doing good and that's it. It's mainly about my grades. So if I go after class, if I go see him, I just ask him if I can see my grade. And if it's not what I want, I ask him why did I get that, but it's nothing other than that. It's just teacher–school business, that's it.

Math created the biggest challenge to cruising through school without trouble. "I get in trouble a lot because I don't do the work, like I sometimes do the work and sometimes I don't."

Kylee did not participate in school activities. When I asked why she thought students participated in school activities she shrugged. "I don't really know," she had a puzzled look on her face, "Sports, maybe they think that's gonna be their career goal later on as a career or it might look good on college applications or something, or their just doing it as a hobby or something." She did not have friends who were involved in extracurricular activities. Near the end of this study she joined Women with a Vision, which met the last Saturday of each month for a semester. "I guess they are there to help us, like teach us how to look for a job, how to apply for a job, and how to pick a job, and how to dress for a job and everything like that," she adjusted her glasses, "My friend told me. She told me cause it is for community service hours and I get 25 hours and I haven't done my community hours [required for graduation] so it was giving me a boost." She did not plan to continue the activity after she received the necessary number of service hours.

Future aspirations

Kylee had mixed views of high school, "I like school, it's fun, but it's boring too when nobody's there with me. But other than that, it is okay. I like to learn." She enjoyed the social aspects of school, but did not pay much attention to the academic side until last year. "I think it is important," Kylee went on to explain how her friends viewed school, "like other people don't think it is important and I didn't used to think it was important, but then high school hit me." Kylee had begun thinking about her future. "I want to become everything," Kylee's eyes lit up as she spoke, "like pediatric nurse, I want to help the homeless, and I want to become a cop or something. I don't want to be one thing. I don't know what I really, really want." When I asked her to explain what she will need to do to reach her goals, she sighed,

> I think it's going to college. I really want to go to college. Like everybody's saying the higher degree you got the easier it is to live life, and so that's how I see it. I just want to go to college because of that, I want to be able to live my life the way I want to live and don't have to worry about anything, so that's pretty much what college means to me. I want be able to live in . . . not a big house, but big enough for me, and my mom, maybe (laughs) and be able to pay bills and not have to worry about money or nothing. I want to have nice cars or whatever, not nice cars but nice enough cars for me and I like to help other people, and I want to have enough money to help my other family members that need money or whatever. That's how I think of living life.

She expressed interest in earning a Master's degree. "I don't really know what a Master's degree is, I know it's a ticket to living a better life," she pushed her glasses up on her nose and looked at the wall, "I don't know what it really means, I need to know what that means. I know you have to go to college a lot and you get other degrees before you get a Master's." I asked what she needed to do between the current semester in high school and getting admitted to college. She shrugged, "Start paying attention more and do what I need to do, trying to work harder than what I am now." She assumed that if she passed her high school classes she could go to college. In her view college and financial aid applications occurred after high school graduation.

Kylee lived in a merged residence that encouraged attendance, but did not necessarily have the resources she needed to achieve academic success. Kylee attended the Women with a Vision meetings once a month; however, she still did not understand the college application process and assumed that college preparation took place at the end of her senior year. She had a C average and had not taken the California High School Exit Exam (CAHSEE) at the conclusion of her junior year in high school. Her guidance counselor advised her not to take the exam because she had sophomore-level credits. Kylee was uncertain how close she was to graduation, but did not take steps to investigate this issue. She shared her philosophy on life, "I think you should just go out and do what you want and like not let anybody hold you back, go out and have fun. Life is too short. Live how you want and don't care."

7

MARCO PLANS TO BE AVERAGE

"Tell me about living in this house with your aunt's family," I ask during our second interview.

"There are just more people, we are family, we treat each other like brothers and sisters," Marco shrugs his shoulders, "It is like the difference between a little and big family."

Marco has a thin frame with hunched shoulders and his short dark hair lacks regular maintenance unless a special event warrants a haircut. His parents were born in Mexico, but he does not necessarily identify with his Mexican heritage. His oldest cousin chastises Marco for not speaking Spanish fluently. Marco stands 5'9", but tells people he is 6'1". His inflated sense of self bleeds into most aspects of life. Although he borders on arrogant, his carefree attitude and harmless sarcasm make him likeable. Similar to Kylee, the structure of his residence encourages participation in school.

Marco lives in a four-bedroom house on the edge of Watts and South Central (see Figure 7.1). The living room has pictures of the family adorning the bookshelves and two gray couches face a 32" flat-screen television. A "Promising Future Leader" plaque his cousin, Lewie, received from the school district stands next to a picture of him at high school graduation. His older cousin, Aaron, also has a shelf dedicated to his high school and college graduation. Aaron moved back home after graduating from college to save money while working in an entry-level position for a company selling airline supplies. A 24" by 36" picture of Marco's sister wearing a long, white quinceñera dress hangs next to the fireplace. Inside the fireplace are numerous candles with images of Catholic saints. Trophies won from school sports line the top of the bookcase.

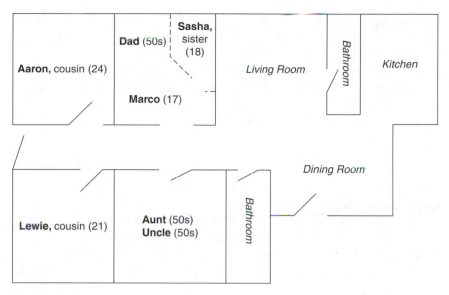

FIGURE 7.1 Marco's house

Much of the house has hardwood floors, though Marco's room has linoleum tile. The room Marco shares with his father and sister is considerably more crowded and darker than the other rooms in the home. A 10" television sits on the dresser with coins, bits of paper, bottle caps and other random items that have been emptied from his father's pockets at the end of each day. Marco was the easiest of the four youth to contact. He has a phone and responds quickly to text messages. We had a standing appointment on Saturday mornings to play volleyball with my friends, which allowed me to speak with him about his week for an hour as we drove to and from the beach. Also, this time served as a point of contact with his residence. I was invited to participate in family events including a birthday and graduation party.

A day in the life of Marco

Morning

At 5:00 the first alarm goes off in his aunt's bedroom followed soon after by his father's alarm clock. Both work at different industrial factories near downtown. His aunt earns the highest income of the adults in the home and serves as a strict disciplinarian. His father and aunt prepare for their day without talking or wasting time. Marco's aunt and father make their lunches and leave for work by 5:30. The house is quiet again for an hour. His uncle and cousins will wake after Marco has left for school. At 6:30 Sasha, Marco's 18-year-old sister, rolls out of bed and heads to the shower. Her section of the room is divided by a 5' high wall with a curtain serving as the door and has just enough space for a single bed, dresser and small computer stand. Fast food cups and clothes cover the minimal floor space. She returns to the room 20 minutes later and gets ready for school. Last fall was her first semester at the University of California in Riverside. She took full advantage of the social aspects of college, but neglected her coursework. Near the end of the semester she was arrested for underage drinking and her family decided to have her move home to attend a community college. The transition back to the family home came with a curfew and restrictions that Sasha has had a difficult time following.

Marco's alarm goes off and he hits the snooze without opening his eyes. He will ignore the alarm one more time before getting out of bed. He shares the other half of the room with his father. Two frequently unmade beds sit on parallel walls with a dresser in between. The poorly lit room lacks order. Marco finally pulls himself out of bed and walks slowly into the bathroom while his sister finishes her makeup at her desk. He comes back into the room and puts on a polo shirt and khaki pants. Chico, the family Chihuahua who wears a blue sweater, runs from his bed to his sister's in a continuous cycle, pausing occasionally when given attention. The dog became part of the family a few years ago after his cousin found him under a car.

Marco pours a glass of water in the kitchen and then sits on the couch. Chico jumps into his lap. "Let's go," his sister's voice cracks. She puts everything she will need for the day into her backpack. Sasha opens the front door and begins to walk out. She pauses and looks at her brother who is still sitting on the couch, "Come on, hurry up." Marco's lack of urgency remains. He grabs an apple to eat on the way to school and then pats Chico on the head before going into his room to get his backpack. A few minutes after 7:30 they get into his sister's car. She drops him off at school, then battles traffic to get to the community college by 9:00.

Daytime

Marco passes two men standing at the school entrance wearing yellow security coats. Barred gates that resemble a prison will be closed and locked the majority of the day. The overcrowded high school has three academies on different tracks that do not interact. One is a diploma track; another supports college-bound students; and the final academy serves students who are missing credits needed for graduation. Each academy has different uniforms. Marco's green polo signifies that he is on a diploma track.

He arrives to class a few minutes late. The art teacher pauses and watches Marco who offers a sly smile as he sits at the studio table shared with three other students. Today they have a choice of drawing a snake, alligator or shark. Marco chooses the snake, which he assumes will be the easiest of the three. He transitions between working on the art project and talking to the others at the table as the teacher wanders around the classroom offering suggestions to students individually. Near the end of class time, his teacher asks for everyone's attention, "You have five minutes to clean up your area and put away your supplies."

Marco wanders slowly through the hallway, occasionally nodding at friends. His history teacher hands him a sheet of paper as Marco walks into the room. The half sheet of paper has five words associated with today's lesson. Marco sits down, turns to the back of the textbook and copies the definitions for each word. The teacher goes over the answers before lecturing for 30 minutes about Martin Luther King and the Civil Rights Movement. Students take notes and ask or answer an occasional question. She passes out a homework assignment with 10 minutes remaining. Marco works through the multiple-choice questions and puts the finished homework in his backpack as the bell rings.

Marco walks to his Advanced Placement (AP) English class without seeing any of his friends during the transition. A worksheet placed on each desk has questions about Chapter 4 of *The Great Gatsby*. Five minutes after class starts the teacher goes over the worksheet and the class participates in a discussion of the text. Halfway through class, the teacher tells students to get into their reading circles, "Discuss how symbolism is used in the Chapter 4." The students make five small circles with their desks. Marco forgot to read the text, but assumes that if he listens closely he will be able to add something to the discussion. This weekend he will try to catch up on the assigned reading. "Alright," the teacher interrupts the group conversations, "I want everyone to put the desks back in rows." The students shuffle seats back to their original locations. "Please take out a piece of paper and write for the next five minutes. The writing prompt is on the board. And do not forget, you have one more chapter to read tonight." Marco draws from the group discussion to answer the question.

Marco's next class is digital art. Half of the computers are already occupied when he arrives, so he sits next to a girl he has known for a few years. "What's up?" he asks while logging on his MySpace account to check for messages. She smiles and points to her computer screen, "Look at this picture from my birthday party Friday night." As the bell rings the teacher walks to the center of the room, "Today you are going to continue working on your Photoshop assignments that are due next week." Most students ignore the announcement and spend the hour browsing the Web, checking email, or managing their MySpace pages. Marco sends a few messages to his friends and looks for a new profile picture. He assumes that he will be able to finish the assignment the day before it is due.

He then goes to his Latin history class. As class begins the teacher passes out a short article about Gaza for students to read silently at their desks. After ten minutes his teacher clears her throat to get the students' attention, "Now I would like you to break up into groups of four and discuss what you would do to improve the situation." Marco joins three people who are near him. "Maybe we should just bomb them," Marco jokes. They discuss their high school soccer team's championship hopes and occasionally comment on the article. A consensus is reached: their soccer team will probably lose in the semifinal game and diplomacy would benefit Gaza. The latter of the two is decided quickly after the teacher writes "diplomacy" on the board. During the final ten minutes of class the small groups share their ideas.

Marco finds a few guys from the volleyball team who already have started eating lunch. "What's up?" Marco sets his tray down and joins the conversation about practice. "Yeah, we been running a lot," Marco shakes his head, "My legs be killing me." One of his friends nods, "Yeah, I am a bit sore too. But it gets better when coach lets us start scrimmaging. I get bored with the drills." The conversation drifts into silence for a moment as they eat. A few minutes later the bell rings. "See ya at practice," Marco nods to the group before walking down the hall alone.

After lunch, Marco heads to his college preparation class. The students, each of whom have identified a scholarship they are eligible to receive, work on writing essays required as part of the application process. The teacher passes back drafts, "I would like each of you to spend time today working on this essay and have a partner give you feedback." Marco works on an essay about a mentor in his life. He has chosen his cousin, Aaron.

After school, Marco lingers in his college preparation class. After the other students have left he pauses at his teacher's desk, "I wanted to let you know that I decided to go to CSUN next year." His teacher, an alumnus of California State University in Northridge (CSUN), smiles, "That is awesome, I think you are really going to like it there." They talk for a few minutes about the campus. "Well, I should be getting to practice. See ya tomorrow," Marco shakes the teacher's hand.

He changes into gym clothes for volleyball practice. Today the coach runs the team through several drills in order to refine the starting lineup; the first game is in two weeks. Practice ends at 5:00. "Alright, see you guys tomorrow," the coach walks into his office. "My legs are killing me," Marco rubs his thighs. His friend, who has been on the team for two years, laughs as they walk into the locker room. Marco puts his backpack on and picks up his gym bag. He decides to stop at the liquor store to buy a candy bar and a soda on the way home.

Evening

Marco lets himself into the house. No one is home. He drops his backpack on his bed and sits down at his computer to check his MySpace page, but there are no new messages. He decides to play video games on his computer while he is waiting for his aunt to make dinner. Nearly two hours pass without him moving from the computer. His dad, who arrives a few minutes later, puts his lunchbox in the kitchen before coming into the bedroom. He nods at his son. "Hey," Marco returns his attention to the video game on his computer. His dad walks to the liquor store a block away before spending the next hour sitting on the porch drinking a beer with a friend from down the street.

At 6:00 his aunt arrives home from work. Marco and Chico come out of the bedroom. "How was your day?" she asks. "Fine," Marco sits at the kitchen table; Chico jumps on his lap. His aunt and Marco chat sporadically as she cooks dinner and cleans the kitchen. She browns hamburger in a frying pan before adding tomato sauce. Aaron, his oldest cousin, opens the front door and smiles, "Hey, what's up."

"Nothing," Marco shrugs. Aaron returns to the dining room after putting his things in his bedroom. "Okay," his aunt motions toward the kitchen, "dinner is ready." Marco eats two plates of spaghetti with his cousin and aunt. The remaining food is left on the kitchen counter; his father, uncle and sister will eat later.

After dinner, Marco goes into Aaron's room to play video games for the next hour. "Did you turn in all that shit for school?" Aaron asks during a pause in the game. "No, I still got some questions," Marco is unsure how to finish the Free Application for Federal Student Aid forms. A few minutes later Marco scores the winning touchdown. "Ha," Marco points toward Aaron, "I told you I was gonna win." Aaron shakes his head, "Whatever, go get those forms, I gotta leave soon." Aaron helps Marco answer the questions about parental income. "Make sure to turn this in tomorrow," Aaron states in a stern tone, "I mean it, this is really important." Marco promises to stop by his college counselor's office in the morning to get her approval before submitting the form.

At 8:00, Aaron heads over to his girlfriend's house. Marco sits at the computer in his sister's side of the room to write a short essay for his English class. He stops writing when he hits three pages—the minimum required length—and prints the document without reviewing what he has read. After putting the paper in his backpack, Marco returns to the game on his computer, which is briefly interrupted each time he receives a text message from a friend. At 11:00, his friend Pedro calls. They chat for a few minutes about a girl Pedro likes and his newly formed band. "Hey, my cousin's havin' a party this weekend, what are you up to?" Marco inquires. "Nothing," his friend pauses, "What time?" Marco gives details about the party before returning to playing video games after the phone call. He gets bored a few minutes before midnight and decides to go to bed.

Weekend

Marco wakes up on Saturday to the sound of his sister and aunt laughing. He walks down the hallway toward the front door wearing flannel pajama pants and a T-shirt. Party supplies had been delivered by a rental company earlier in the morning. A white party tent covers the parking spaces, which also serve as the basketball court. Sasha and her aunt are designing the table arrangements to maximize space. "Do you need help?" Marco squints and puts his hand up to block the sun. His aunt instructs him to set up the tables as his sister puts six chairs at each. The remainder of the day is spent preparing food and decorations for Lewie's 21st birthday party.

Guests begin arriving at 6:00. Members of their extended family, specifically those with small children, arrive first. Loud Spanish music booms from the large speakers that have been borrowed from Lewie's friend who is a deejay. Marco's dad and uncle sit with a couple of friends at one of the tables; each man holds a bottle of liquor he brought to share. By 7:00 the men have difficulty walking to the keg without stumbling.

Aaron, Lewie, Sasha and Marco come out of the house as guests their age begin to arrive. Sasha, wearing a short black dress that hugs her slender frame, carries a tray of Jello shots. She makes a round every 30 minutes throughout the night with different flavors. Aaron, Lewie and Marco have a similar style: a pressed button-up shirt, baggy jeans, white tennis shoes and freshly cut and meticulously styled short hair. They sit at a table in the center of the tent. A few college friends of both cousins, including both of their girlfriends, join the party. Sasha leans over the table, "I made a few different kinds of shots. This one is margarita flavored. Here try it." Each person takes a shot. She takes a break from serving and joins the table. Although weather had been unseasonably warm during the day, the temperature begins to drop after dark. Marco and Aaron ask his sister if she is cold. The plunging neckline of the spaghetti strap dress offers minimal protection from the cooling temperature. "No, really, I don't even have chicken skin," she holds her arms up as evidence. Aaron pours Sasha a beer and sets it on the table in front of her, "But I am cutting you off at four beers this time. We are not going to have another night like last time." She smiles and takes a sip of the beer. The friends at the table joke about the New Year's Eve party Aaron hosted. Aaron points at one of his friends, "You got so drunk you fell in the front yard and almost hit your head." "Nah," the stout Hispanic man in his 20s smiles sheepishly, "I did not pass out. I decided to lay down because I was afraid I might throw up." "Whatever you fool, you almost knocked out your teeth," Aaron emphasizes each word. "No, really," his friend defends himself, "I walked outside and thought I needed to lay down. I remember everything you all said." Lewie jumps into the conversation, "Shut up, you was drunk out of your mind." Everyone laughs. The friend smiles as he sips his beer.

Marco's aunt prepared the side dishes for dinner, but hired two women to make tacos for guests. Throughout dinner the guests yell to be heard over the combination of Mariachi and Spanish pop music. The music drowns out the usual sounds of the neighborhood including planes flying in for landing, sirens, squealing tires and people talking on the street. Four different groups form at the party. Marco's aunt entertains the extended family in one corner; Aaron and Lewie sit with their college friends in the center of the tent; Marco's dad and uncle drink with two men near the keg; and another group around Lewie's age wearing T-shirts and smoking stand in the driveway. The men sitting with Marco's father are no longer able to stand; one has his head on the table with his eyes nearly closed as his hand grasps a bottle of rum. Although a party was going on around them, they rarely interact with others.

Sasha begins another round of Jello shots. Marco and Pedro, his friend from high school, take a shot each time she visits their table. Pedro, who recently completed his diploma at an alternative education center, now works at Starbucks in a neigh-boring community. He pats Marco on the shoulder, "Give me a few more months and I will hopefully be a shift lead and you can get a job there, I will hire you." Marco nods, but has no intentions to get a job. "Are you still in that band?" Lewie asks as the two boys swallow a green shot. "My band has a gig coming up in Long Beach," Pedro explains to Lewie, "You would like it, we play like all kinds of genres of rock music. Marco wants to come; you should stop by and see it." Pedro tried to get another band off the ground a few months ago, but it crumbled after a disagreement between members. "Alright," Lewie nods, "maybe I will."

A large Hispanic man with a baggy white T-shirt and jeans arrives carrying a binder and laptop computer. An oversized gold chain with a cross hangs from his neck. Lewie and Aaron greet him with a hug and walk over to the speakers on the porch. At 8:30, Aaron grabs the microphone, "Can I have everyone's attention. We are here to celebrate my brother, Lewie's birthday. Here you go Lewie." Lewie smiles as he takes the microphone, "Thank you guys all for coming out tonight. Let's have a party." Everyone claps and cheers. Sasha appears behind the two men with a cake and candles. As the crowd finishes singing "Happy Birthday," Lewie cuts the first piece of the cake and smiles in an exaggerated manner for a photo with his brother. Sasha takes this opportunity to smear frosting on Lewie's face. He laughs and acts as though he is going to return the favor as Sasha runs off. Most people miss the incident because their attention has returned to the conversations at their table.

At 9:00, Aaron takes the microphone again and the music stops, "Alright you all, it is time to start dancing." His friends cheer. Aaron nods, "So all you all that are sitting at these tables here need to move so we can have a dance floor. So what I am saying is you all need to get the fuck up and move." The audience laughs. As he finishes, Britney Spears's latest song comes on. The music shifts from Spanish to English for the remainder of the night. The guests dance under the full moon and clear sky until 2:00 in the morning; however, fewer family members remain as more college friends arrive.

Reflecting on risk and protective factors

Marco, a naturally confident teenager, enjoyed socializing with both friends and family. His home had less conflict than Isaac and Juan experienced. The residential context allowed him to build close relationships with family members who valued and participated in the educational process. Marco had close relationships with family members who attended college. Unlike the other residences, not every family in his home was technically doubled-up. His father sought refuge in the home of his sister; however, she did not rely on his financial contributions. Below I share the risk and protective aspects of his life that influenced his decision to pursue a college education.

Residential history and context

Marco was born in Hollywood. His family rented a three-bedroom apartment in South Central Los Angeles. His parents had the largest bedroom; his sister and he had their own rooms. A disruption to the family's residential stability occurred when Marco was in 1st grade. Similar to Kylee, his parents' divorce was the impetus.

Marco initially moved with his mother and sister to Mexico. He had a difficult time adjusting to the new environment because he could only speak conversational Spanish. He got into several physical fights with boys at school during the year he lived in Tijuana. His mother decided she needed a change and no longer wanted the responsibility of raising her two children. According to Marco, the switch happened after a phone conversation between his parents, "I think we met in Tijuana and we went with my dad and never went back with my mom." His father had moved in with his sister's family after his wife and children left. Marco and his sister joined his father; the three of them began sharing one room in his aunt's home. Marco moved several times in a short period when he was in elementary school, but he experienced residential stability throughout middle and high school. The two households lived together for nearly a decade. "We were living with my aunt and they decided to buy a house," Marco explained. His father agreed to rent one of the bedrooms.

The extended family merged into one household with his aunt as the matriarch of the home. When I asked him to describe his relationship with the other residents, he looked puzzled, "We are family. We treat each other like brothers and sisters." He described his aunt, who formed a parental relationship with her niece and nephew, as "Like my mom, she has lived with me for more than half my life, she's like the authority figure. I got to ask her if I want to go somewhere, if she says yes, then my dad will probably say yes, but sometimes he says no." She coordinated the home, including organization of meals and setting expectations for behavior for the entire residence.

Although the two families have lived in the same residence for ten years, the tenuous stability of the arrangement for Marco's immediate family was made evident halfway through the study. During the second interview, the large picture of his sister was missing from the wall and had been placed behind the television facing the wall. All the pictures of his sister were removed from the bookcase. Marco took a deep breath and shook his head:

> She's not living here anymore. Over the weekend, you know how she got arrested for underage drinking and stuff, they brought her home, and for two months she needs to go to AA meetings, like the judge told her that. She went like, it was like Friday or Thursday, and she went and then like at 11:00 or 11:30 my dad told me to call her and see where she at and when she coming home. I was like, "When you coming home?" And she was like, "The lady is still talking to me." I was like, "The lady don't stay until 11:30," right? They usually end the meetings at like 10:00 or before, and she was like, "You don't believe me?" And I said no, she said she would be home later. It was like 1:30 and she sent me a text that said she was not coming home no more, she was going back to Riverside.

Sasha had become accustomed to making her own decisions and enjoyed the freedom associated with being away in college. Moving back in the home after getting arrested for drinking was difficult. The curfew created the most frustration. She started violating her aunt's rules. The tension finally led to a family conflict. "Oh," Marco's eyes widened, "then the crazy thing happened this weekend, it was craziest shit ever." His sister came to the house on a Sunday evening, after being gone for two days, with a police officer as an escort. Marco's eyes widened as he explained what happened:

> The cop came in and he was like, "We are here so she can take her stuff." So she went into her room and took all her stuff, and then my aunt was crying and she was like, "You ain't part of this family no more, I never want to see you again. I hope we never hear of you." And then Aaron did too, and then Lewie did too, and then my dad, I don't know, he was sad or something.

The home was normally structured and peaceful when I was around. I asked why his sister brought a police officer. Marco thought that Sasha brought an officer to the house because she was afraid "that someone was gonna smack the shit out of her or something." Lewie told Sasha that she was ungrateful for all the things his mother had done for her. Sasha left the home and did not return during the remaining months of the study. She moved in with a few friends and had minimal contact with her family.

Marco's dad had a hard time watching his daughter struggle in college and then move out of the home. When I asked why Marco thought his dad was sad, he lowered his eyes, "Cause my mom did the same thing, she left him and stuff, and then my sister left him too." The house returned to its natural order. "I guess we move on now, they took her pictures off the living room wall already," Marco shrugged his shoulders, "My aunt doesn't want to talk to her ever again."

Social network

Marco spent the majority of his time outside of school with his family, specifically his two cousins. Aaron was the first in the family to go to college; however, Marco's father and aunt both graduated from high school. In 2007, Aaron graduated from the University of California in San Diego. He encouraged his younger brother and two cousins to work hard in high school so they could attend college. In particular, he wanted them to get admitted to a school in the University of California system. "I forgot to take the [ACT subject test]," Marco admitted, "so I am kinda a disappointment, I ended up getting into a Cal State." Marco looked up to his cousin and considered him "Like my brother, he is a role model, I guess." Aaron was an educational resource and example for the entire residence. Marco went to Aaron if he had a question about homework, for example, "Like two weeks ago, it was an essay, it was *Frankenstein*, I think, and some other book. He reads it over and tells me what to do to improve it, like what it is missing."

His younger cousin, Lewie, was in his second year of college at California State University in Los Angeles. Marco looked up to him, but in a different way. Lewie's participation in college qualified him as a role model, but it was "not the same cause he has not graduated yet." Marco viewed Lewie more as a peer, "We talk about everything, like games, girls and all that stuff."

Sasha served as an example of what Marco wanted to avoid. She failed to complete the first semester at the University of California in Riverside. Marco disapproved of her attitude towards school, "She is lazy, I guess. She sleeps every day. I feel like kicking her sometimes. I throw Chico at her and he starts biting her and she wakes up." When I asked if she was a role model, he gasped, "Not really, cause she slacks on responsibility. She is not used to being so free."

Marco also socialized outside of the house. He had four friends who he had known for several years. Pedro was the same age as Marco, but chose to get his GED after finding out that he was not on track to earn a diploma. He worked at Starbucks to pay the bills while investing the majority of his time trying to get his rock band off the ground. The two began to drift apart during Marco's senior year as their lives took different paths; however, Marco went to see Pedro's band play a couple of times a year and they frequently send text messages to each other. His other friends attended school and had postsecondary aspirations. Cecilia, a friend for nearly eight years, planned to attend college after graduation. According to Marco, "She thinks school is important. She has pretty good grades, like a 3.7 or something." Abraham and Victor, also known as "the drivers" for social events, attended school regularly, but were less concerned about grades. Marco described Abraham, who looks like the "salsa guy" on the hot sauce container, as interested in "passing his classes, but he hasn't decided about where to go to college yet." And Victor "has red hair, that is like his natural hair, that is weird, right? He plays soccer for school, he is passing all of his classes, has one B. He is going to a Cal State." The group of friends went to the movies or a fast food restaurant once a month. When I asked if he spoke about college with his friends, Marco laughed, "We talk about other stuff." The topics of conversations generally concerned pop culture or relationships between their friends.

Educational factors

Marco has had the most stable schooling environment of the youth who participated in the study. Early in elementary school he moved frequently; however, he attended one middle and high school. Although the location was stable, he missed school once a week. As he explained, the days he skipped were leisure,

> I got up, went to my computer, turned it on, then logged on, then I went and brushed my teeth, then I went and played some 360 in my brother's room, I got bored so I turned it off, I went back to my computer and started playing a game, and then I got bored from that so I started watching

TV in the living room, I got bored from watching TV, so I started playing with Chico.

He laughed while explaining what happened when he arrived late to school. "I usually get detention or something, but I never go," he smirked. "I got connections. I know people. I know the highest ranks, like vice principal and teachers and staff and they just mark me off detention." The high school endured overcrowding, limited resources and gang violence. In 2007, the public high school converted to a charter school run by Green Dot after being identified as low performing for several years. The administration struggled to manage the students and school.

However, he faced consequences at home for missing school. His aunt and Aaron expected regular school attendance and at least passing grades. I asked him what would happen when they found out he skipped school. He shook his head, "[My aunt and cousin] say, 'Why didn't you go to school? You better go to school tomorrow or I am gonna kick your ass.'" As punishment, he lost his video games or phone for a couple of days.

Marco's relationships with his teachers varied. He had a few key relationships that encouraged his postsecondary ambitions, including his AP English teacher who created a rigorous learning environment. "She doesn't give us the same work every day, she mixes it up," he explained, "She gives us a lot of homework and doesn't let us do it in class. She says that homework is home work." He went to her for advice concerning coursework, personal issues and college preparation. Marco gave an example of their interactions, "Sometimes I go to her after class, I go in to ask for help and then we just talk. School wise, she tells me how I can make my writing better." Also, she appreciated his sarcasm. "I called her coldhearted too," Marco had a proud tone as he spoke, "cause she didn't let me take a test cause I was three minutes late and she told me I couldn't take it. I was like, 'you're coldhearted.' And ever since I have called her that." His college readiness class focused on the process of preparing for and applying to postsecondary institutions:

> The teacher is pretty nice. He went to Northridge. I be asking him about Northridge and he tells me. He is the one that told me about the new rooms and what there is to do over there. He wants me to go to college. He says that I shouldn't slack off.

When I asked why this teacher's advice matters, Marco responded in a matter-of-fact tone, "Cause he has been through it." The remaining teachers he either had no relationship with or an adversarial relationship. He was sent to the office "a couple of times for talking to my teachers. They said I was being a smart ass, I was using big words." Marco laughed,

> I was being smart. They would ask me a question and I answer them with a smart answer. They said I was being rude. I went to the office and they asked

"What did you do?" and I said nothing. And they told me to sit down and I went to the next class.

Marco also participated in extracurricular activities. He participated in sports; however, he was on different teams each year. Over the four years of high school he spent a season on the soccer, baseball, volleyball, basketball and golf teams. "I just like seeing if I can do it," he smiled. Marco enjoyed the social aspects of sports, but did not fully commit to the teams or connect with the coaches. After two months on the volleyball team during his senior year Marco quit the team.

Future aspirations

His initial response to how school fit into his life was, "It makes up eight hours of my day." His view of education shifted when he discussed his long-term goals. "[School] matters," he smiled, "You get more money and you will not have to work so hard, and better job and you're smarter too. If you are smarter you can use people. Like manipulate them." When I asked if he wanted to manipulate people, he smiled, "If I have to, yeah. To get my goal." He had not decided on a career, but was considering nursing, computer programming or criminal justice. He explained what he needed to do to reach his goals, "Well, you need to get accepted to college first, which I did that already. You need to finish high school, like not failing any classes, I still need to do that. You got pick the right program and you got to stay on track in college."

He was confident that nothing would inhibit his ability to succeed. During one interview I asked him what grades he expected to receive in college. "Not straight As, passing," Marco laughed, "Passing is the same as an A. Cause you will pass either way, am I right?" When I told him a difference existed, he raised one eyebrow as he smirked and shook his head, "Nah uh." His current grades were "pretty good," he explained:

> Like a 3.4 or 3.5. My overall is a 3.1, but that is cause of one semester, but as soon as I finish this semester it will be up to like at 3.5. Last semester I didn't go to school at all. I don't know, I got bored, it was no challenge. If I don't feel challenges I will miss school to make it challenges. I won't go to school for like two days to try and make it challenging. Cause if my grades drop, I have to make it up, that is challenging.

Kylee and Marco both lived in merged residences that limited conflict and encouraged educational participation. However, outcomes differed. Marco applied to four institutions in the California State University system. He was accepted to all of them, but decided to attend California State University in Northridge. Aaron assisted Marco through the process and encouraged him to learn from Sasha's mistake. He submitted federal financial aid forms and CalGrant materials. Although he had not visited the campus, he met with a college preparation teacher frequently to ask questions and get information about Northridge. Marco felt confident that he would do fine in college.

PART III
Analysis and Implications[1]

The vignettes in the previous sections provided a sense of how youth structured their time and the influence of each residential context. The structure of the residences and social networks of the youth shaped how they participated in the educational process. The chaos of Isaac's residential situation further distanced him from the educational process. The lack of consequences for failing to attend school discouraged him from actively participating in school. He engaged in substance abuse and spent considerable time with friends who were involved in high-risk behaviors. Juan's residence was similarly chaotic. He escaped conflict by engaging in academics and sports. Attending college was viewed as a path out of this environment for Juan.

The lack of structure Isaac and Juan experienced differed dramatically from the homes of Kylee and Marco. Kylee was expected to attend school consistently. The two mothers intentionally structured the residence to ensure their children attended school. Marco lived in a structured residence that supported and reinforced his educational aspirations. Not a highly motivated student, Marco continued to persist through high school and apply to college under the supervision of his aunt and cousin. Marco and Kylee lived in structured environments that encouraged educational participation; however, the relationships they had with friends, family and teachers differed.

The remaining chapters highlight aspects of the participants' residential context, social network influences and educational experiences that contributed to their educational resilience. I discuss how the structure of these residences influenced their participation in the educational process as well as exploring why the youth achieved different educational outcomes.

Note

1 See Hallett (2010) and Hallett (forthcoming). Portions of these articles have been revised and included in Chapters 8 and 9.

8

INFLUENCE OF RESIDENTIAL STRUCTURE

"Faith hasn't been yelling at me for a long time really, since we moved here. She doesn't have nothing to yell at me for cause I'm not here," Isaac explains.

"Why aren't you here?" I inquire.

"Cause to avoid problems, something bad is always happening here, or something comes up stolen here, they're always arguing here, it's always something," he shrugs, "and I don't want to be a part of it, so I don't have to get blamed for nothing."

The stories presented in the previous chapters offer a glimpse into the lives of four youth living doubled-up and the influence their residential arrangements had on their educational participation. Isaac had a vague long-term goal of becoming a professional athlete or firefighter, but the daily choices he made to escape the chaos of his living environment resulted in educational disengagement. Although Kylee's residence valued attending school and treating teachers with respect, aspects of her network limited her access to information about the educational process. Marco and Juan both intended to enroll in college the fall after high school graduation and took steps to bring this goal to fruition; however, their residences differed in the level of support for postsecondary aspirations. The differing experiences illustrate the complexity of urban life. Although I focus on the residential influences in this chapter, two additional points are worth noting. First, these youth did not define themselves by their residential arrangements. Rather, their identity was shaped by the relationships, interests and experiences that happened within and outside of the home. None of the youth identified with the terms *doubled-up* or *homeless*. Second, themes emerged from the data that helped explain how youth experienced doubled-up residences, but a singular definition of a doubled-up residence was not evident.

This study grew out of the desire to better understand how residential instability influences educational participation. I use a resilience framework to make sense of the experiences of the youth. As aforementioned, I define educational resilience as actively engaging in school and academic activities that enable an individual who may be at risk of dropping out to complete a high school diploma and transition to postsecondary education.

Employing different models of resilience

The youth who participated in this study lived in overcrowded residences in low-income neighborhoods. The schools in these areas had low levels of graduation and the communities had high rates of crime. Although the residential contexts have many similarities, Isaac and Kylee had difficulty completing the requirements for high school graduation whereas Marco and Juan were in the process of transitioning to a university. Some may ask why four youth living in similar situations had different outcomes. Resiliency Theory provides a framework for understanding how factors within the lives of these individuals interact and result in different experiences. Before considering these factors in detail, I want to briefly discuss the four models of resilience: Invincibility, Compensatory, Challenge and Protective. Researchers generally ascribe to one of the models and ignore the other three. In the section that follows, I review data from the current study to determine how each model might explain the experiences of youth living doubled-up.

The *Invincibility Model* assumes that some youth are invincible and others are vulnerable. These innate qualities determine how an individual will respond to adverse situations. This model would suggest that Juan and Marco possessed innate resilience whereas Isaac and Kylee were vulnerable. This perspective has been discredited by researchers who argue that aspects of the youth and environment better explain outcomes than innate qualities. The participants faced similar risks associated with crowded living conditions, low-performing schools and neighborhood violence; however, the structure of their residences and the access they had to protective factors better explained the differing outcomes than innate predispositions to either success or failure. The difference between Marco attending college and Isaac dropping out of school could be explained by the presence or absence of factors associated with family and network support. Marco actually lacked internal motivation, but had people in his network pushing him. On the other hand, Isaac possessed internal motivation that slowly eroded as obstacles mounted limiting his ability to attend school. The Invincibility Model oversimplified the complexity of the participants' life experiences.

Of the three primary models of resilience, the *Compensatory Model* relies most heavily on quantitative methods. This approach assumes that each factor can be assigned a value. The risk factors are subtracted from the protective factors to determine the likelihood of a positive or negative outcome. The underlying premise that protective factors may compensate for the negative influences of risk factors is relevant to this study. Juan, for example, possessed a high level of internal motivation and was determined to reach his goals. These personality traits allowed him to persist through school even though he faced multiple barriers, including limited family support. The nature of this study made confirming or refuting the utility of the Compensatory Model difficult. A quantitative study that assigns each of the traits a numeric value would better assess the relationships between risk and protective factors.

The *Challenge Model* of resilience suggests that low levels or high levels of a risk factor lead to negative outcomes whereas moderate levels may result in the development of coping strategies that protect the individual from future risk. The exact point where risk shifts to protection varies depending upon the individual and context. Residential mobility functioned in this way. Juan and Marco experienced mobility at a specific point in their lives, which disrupted their social networks. Both of the youth discussed the difficulty of losing and forming friendships during that period. Consistency of their physical residence since that point enabled them to establish and maintain new relationships. Neither developed a coping strategy to deal with moving and, as a result, they were apprehensive about leaving for college. Isaac represented the other end of the spectrum; he had moved multiple times each year since his mother was sent to prison. At some point he lost interest in forming relationships he perceived would be short-term. For each of these youth, movement negatively influenced social network formation. Kylee, on the other hand, developed strategies that enabled her to establish friendships quickly with each transition and limited the fear of social demands at each new school. However, she may be nearing the point where the level of risk becomes too burdensome. When I asked about the possibility of moving again, she responded, "I like the people here, and it is kinda sad that I am just going to be moving again, and that I am going to have to restart all over again, and stuff." Mobility was the only risk factor that was explained by using the Challenge Model.

The *Protective Model* assumes that protective factors have the potential of interacting with risks to limit the negative influence on outcomes. The experiences of Juan and Isaac help illustrate this point. Both of these youth had postsecondary aspirations. They lived in neighborhoods with similar risks, including gang violence and low-performing schools. Their residential contexts involved limited educational support and high levels of conflict. Given their similar situations, why is Juan going to attend UCLA after graduation and Isaac will likely drop out of high school? The peer groups and mentor relationships these youth were involved in helped explain the differing outcomes. Juan's friends were generally engaged in the educational process and encouraged him to pursue his goals whereas Isaac's friends were involved in gangs, used drugs, and dropped out of school. Juan had several mentors encouraging his educational participation. His soccer coach gave him support throughout his high school career and his college mentor helped him navigate the transition to postsecondary education. Isaac's mentor provided sporadic emotional support, but did not focus as much attention on the educational process. As the findings presented throughout this chapter illustrate, the presence of a protective factor helped explain the likelihood of resilience.

I initially used all four of the models to analyze the data. The difference between youth who achieved educational resilience and those who did not could not be explained by innate qualities, but rather by the presence or absence of protective factors. Although the Challenge Model was useful for describing how mobility related to resilience and the Compensatory Model had the potential to understand the interaction between personality and risk factors, the Protective Model was most useful in understanding how the youth in this study developed resilience. The interactions between risk factors (e.g. violence in the neighborhood or substance use) and protective factors (e.g. family structure or a mentor) was related to how youth participated in school and understood the educational process.

This study contributes to the Protective Model of resilience by considering how factors are experienced. The presence of a factor did not necessarily contribute to either risk or protection. Considering how the factor occurred in the participant's life and his or her response was more important than making a list of risk and protective factors. I provide two examples to help illustrate this point. Living in a doubled-up residence—a subcategory of homelessness—is generally considered to be a risk factor. In addition, a mentoring relationship is frequently identified as a protective factor. I elaborate further on each of these factors; however, both had the potential to possess either risk or protective qualities. Was the doubled-up residence structured to support or discourage education? Did the mentor provide educational guidance or sporadic social activities? Simply identifying a factor that occurred oversimplified how these youth developed educational resilience or became disconnected from the educational process.

Influence of living doubled-up

Instability frames the findings presented below. Residential context and the presence of risk or protection were not stagnant factors that could easily be captured by point-in-time data. Previous studies have argued that environments are not static and individuals may respond differently to a factor over time (Deater-Deckard, Ivy & Smith, 2005; Luthar & Cicchetti, 2000; Rutter, 1993). The qualitative case study design enabled me to observe how these factors changed: the structure of Marco's residence shifted when his sister moved out; Juan's knowledge of the college process evolved as he worked with a university mentor; Isaac's physical and emotional distance from school increased when he moved to a new location and became involved with a high-risk peer group; and Kylee joined her first school organization. The inevitability of change was common among all of the participants. Viewing factors as a process enabled me to focus on how the youth experienced life within a doubled-up residence.

In order to understand how the processes at work in the lives of doubled-up youth enhanced or detracted from educational resilience, I discuss broader definitional issues and explore the influence of larger social forces on individual perceptions and actions. The overarching finding is that living doubled-up has the potential to be both a protective and risk factor, but the outcome depends upon the structure of the residence and social network factors outside the home. To justify how I reached this conclusion, I begin by explaining how youth and families defined their residential situation. I then turn to how the social environments within the residences shaped the youth's educational participation. Finally, I outline how the differing residential formations contributed to either protection or risk.

How doubled-up youth defined their social environments

The social environments of the youth primarily involved their residence, school and friends' homes. I expected relationships with extended family outside of the residence and religious organizations to be more prominent. On occasion the youth would mention a member of his or her extended family, but they did not have regular contact with these individuals. In some instances, these relationships had been strained during the initial economic crisis that led to residential instability. Kylee's mother lived with several family members after her divorce; each situation led to conflict that fractured the relationship. Youth who lived with extended family members during the study acknowledge how conflicts could disrupt relationships without carefully managing the residence. Kylee, Juan and Marco identified as Catholic and Isaac consider himself Christian, but none of them attended a church or had consistent interactions with a congregation.

Although relationships formed with peers and educators influenced how participants viewed educational processes, I focused primarily on the residential context. The limited space and economic necessity of living with multiple households in a single residence were shared by all of the youth. How households related to one another and the youth's response to those interactions differed. The view of family, relationship between households, and presence of a decision-maker shaped youth's experiences within their home and how they participated in the educational process. These issues and the influence on educational participation are expanded upon below.

Inclusive view of family

With the exception of Isaac, study participants lived with a biological parent and at least one sibling. During interviews, participants distinguished between individuals within their residence with whom they had biological connections and those they did not; however, the distinctions were less clear when I conducted observations. This ambiguity was most pronounced with Isaac, Kylee and Marco. Isaac thought of Faith as his mother even though they did not have a direct biological connection and he referred to Faith's children as "like brothers and sisters" to him. Kylee also spoke of Angela's two children as her brother and sister. She often took responsibility for babysitting and assisting with their care. During the first interview, Marco explained his biological relationship with each person in the house and spoke about his sister being his only sibling. I was confused during casual conversation when he spoke about his brothers. Marco explained his relationship with his two cousins in a scholarship essay: "My aunt has two sons and I love them as my own brothers because we have lived together for over 12 years and we have gotten used to each other."

Juan did not have a similar affinity for all members of his residence. He took responsibility for his siblings and avoided interactions with others living in the residence. Tension between members of his residence limited the ability of households in Juan's residence to collaborate. He specifically discussed biological connections between individuals in the residence, including his "grandfather, who is not really my grandfather" and his "grandfather's son." The households in his apartment took steps to remain separate. I discuss the relationships between households further in the next section. The more the households collaborated the tighter the bond became, leading to a more expansive view of family.

Merged residence or separate households

Each residence was composed of at least two households. The interaction between households generally took one of two forms: merged residence or separate households. The choices, both intentional and unconscious, concerning the residence's structure influenced how the households managed childrearing and daily responsibilities. Table 8.1 provides a summary of the basic differences between the two residential formations that will be discussed throughout this chapter.

Merged residences occurred when two households blended families, which resulted in shared responsibility for children and division of labor to complete household tasks. The decision to engage in this residential relationship grew out of a desire to achieve a relatively higher standard of living than was possible independently. Kylee and Marco lived in merged residences that each functioned similarly to a single nuclear family. In Kylee's case, the two mothers divided responsibility for raising children, paying bills and managing the home. Each woman took the lead for different aspects of the residence and provided that function for both households. For example, Lucy cared for the children and Angela worked two jobs to pay the bills. This limited the duplication of tasks and allowed the women to have a higher standard of living than they could afford separately as well as strengthened the assumed family bond between their children. These women were able to purchase a vehicle and afford a larger apartment by living together than they previously had independently.

Prior to the current location, Lucy lived in a studio apartment with her three children and Angela shared a bedroom with her two children in a family member's home. The current apartment was crowded, but provided more space than the families' previous locations. Marco's father was unable to afford an apartment independently after his divorce and sought refuge in his sister's home, which

TABLE 8.1 Differing formations within doubled-up residences

	Merged residence	Separate households
Relationship between households	Households functioned as a single unit	Households split rent and utility bills, but other aspects of daily life remained separate
Head of household	One person made decisions for the residence and managed conflicts that could not be easily resolved	One person served as the decision-maker when conflicts arose; however, other residences were suspicious of his or her loyalty to one of the households
Parenting responsibilities	One parent took the lead in providing childcare for all of the youth in the residence	Each family was independently responsible for providing childcare for youth
Household responsibilities	Daily tasks were performed as a single unit, including meals, cleaning and laundry	Daily tasks were the responsibility of each household. Each family prepared a meal, made decisions about cleaning and did laundry
Educational responsibilities	One parent managed educational issues for all households, including homework, school uniforms, and transportation to school	Each family was responsible for meeting educational needs. In general, basic needs took priority over educational participation
Residential stability	Households had emotional and financial connectivity, which encouraged remaining as a single unit	Households remained separate and were willing to consider other residential options

enabled him to benefit from assistance with childcare and his children to live in a larger home with cable and internet access.

The families living in merged residences expected to remain a single unit in the future. Marco's aunt and uncle purchased the home where he lived. His father and aunt agreed to live together indefinitely. The households in Kylee's residence did not have biological connections; however, the two mothers entered contractual obligations together. A few months before the study began they signed a five-year loan for a car. The possibility existed that the families may move from the current location, but both women expected to find a new apartment together. Although the physical location may not be stable, Kylee expected to have consistent relationships within the home.

In separate households, childrearing and managing the home were maintained within each household. This formation allowed individual households to benefit from shared financial responsibility for the home without losing autonomy. The decision to enter this residential formation grew out of economic desperation whereas merged residences also used a shared space to increase their standard of living. Isaac and Juan lived in separate households where families shared responsibility for paying rent and utility bills; however, the households lived alongside each other without collaborating to complete daily tasks. Youth living in separate households did not have the same level of supervision as those in merged residences. The primary caregiver spent additional time making sure basic needs were met and was unable to devote as much attention to monitoring educational participation. Juan monitored the educational participation of his younger sister and brother, but no one in the residence took responsibility for guiding his educational progress. At the end of the study his mother was still unaware that he had been accepted to college. Juan's mother regularly worked two jobs to pay her portion of the bills and provide for her family. The two refrigerators in the kitchen illustrated the level of separation between households. Conflict arose between and within the separate households. Both Isaac and Juan sought refuge outside of the residence. Their social networks, which dramatically differed, influenced how they participated in the educational process and their exposure to risk or protective factors. Juan had a strong network of peers and mentors that encouraged his participation in school and offered emotional support. Isaac's network was disconnected from the educational system and encouraged his participation in behaviors that negatively influenced his engagement in school.

Future unity of the residence was less certain in separate households. The lack of cohesion enabled each of the households to consider other housing options. Two households moved out of Isaac's residence during the study, leaving the remaining residents uncertain how bills would be paid. Juan's family remained in the apartment throughout the study, but he admitted that his mother was interested in finding an alternative living arrangement apart from the other households. The social environment of the shared residences was less stable than the merged households. The youth were uncertain who would be living with them in the future.

All residences, regardless of structure, experienced conflict within and between households. The differing methods of structuring relationships within the residences influenced the level of conflict. The next section discusses how residences handled disagreements.

Presence of a head of household

Each residence had a person who was responsible for discipline, conflict resolution, managing the finances and making decisions concerning the residence. This person coordinated payment of bills and served as the final decision-maker when issues could not be resolved between members of the residence; however, the structure of the residence shaped how this responsibility was exercised. The two merged residences had an authoritarian figure whereas Isaac lived with a weak head of household and Juan's was frequently absent.

The authoritarian head of household in the merged residences made decisions concerning household management and her decisions were considered final. In

Marco's case, the presence of a head of household was evident from the outset. When I asked his father if Marco could participate, he responded, "I don't know." I was referred to his aunt, who allowed Marco to participate in the study after I explained to her the purpose and reviewed the consent forms. Her power in decision-making also surfaced when Sasha, Marco's sister, broke the rules concerning curfew and began drinking while on probation. His aunt made the decision that Sasha had to move out of the house and nearly excommunicated her. Marco and his father did not fully support this decision, but decided not to openly challenge the aunt's decision. In Kylee's case, the presence of a head of household was not immediately apparent, in part because Angela worked two fulltime jobs and was rarely home during the evenings. However, Kylee's mother was clear to note that Angela made decisions for the residence and served as the "man of the house." Lucy got Angela's approval before making decisions concerning the home and the two women frequently discussed the finances for the residence. The youth in both of the merged residences knew they would face consequences if a rule was broken. The head of household enforced the rules, whether or not she was the child's biological parent.

The head of household's role was more complicated in Isaac's and Juan's residences. Instead of making decisions for the entire residence, the head of household had to manage conflict between individuals and families. Accusations of favoritism arose since the person in charge was a member of one of the households and each family functioned with independent goals. In Isaac's case, Faith was reluctant to take an authoritative role. She took responsibility for paying bills and purchasing food for the house; however, remaining decisions were made by the other members of the residence. The residence did not have a clear set of rules that individuals were expected to follow or consequences for not attending school, cleaning the house or coming home at a set time. During the month of January, Isaac spent nearly two weeks with his friends in a Skid Row hotel without asking Faith's permission. She was upset that he disappeared, but he did not face consequences when he returned after a week of drug and alcohol use with friends. The cluttered home and unsanitary conditions in his residence served as a visual representation of the lack of order and collaboration. For all intents and purposes, each person in the household had equal footing when a conflict arose, but a system of resolving disagreements did not exist. Seemingly minor decisions, such as doing the dishes, resulted in heated arguments. I spent four hours in the emergency room with Isaac's stepbrother after he broke a bone in his hand. An argument with his sister about her children messing up his room escalated and he punched a wall. Unlike the merged residences, the head of household did not take an active role in preventing and managing conflict.

Juan's residence functioned somewhere in between the authoritarian households of Kylee and Marco and the weak head of household in Isaac's home. Juan's grandmother was the central figure in the home and made major decisions, such as ensuring bills were paid and determining who lived in the apartment. Her role was muted by her limited presence in the home. She lived with her employer four nights a week and, during her absence, the residence functioned similarly to Isaac's home; however, she attempted to rein in conflict on the weekends. Juan felt this led to strategic engagement in conflict and manipulation, because his grandmother had to make decisions based upon information given to her after the fact. Tension existed between his aunt, his grandfather's son, and Juan's family. Although his grandmother attempted to resolve conflict, animosity built up in her absence. Juan felt that his grandfather took his aunt's side in most conflicts, "He doesn't seem to care as much about us as my aunt. Our room could need to be painted and he won't tell the owner, but if it be my aunt, he would go and tell the landlord immediately." He tried to keep his siblings in the bedroom and avoided contact with the other members of the residence. "I just try to keep it cool with everybody and don't get into the way of my aunt," he explained, "I just do my things and stay out of the way."

The social environments of the youth varied depending on the structure of the residence and how conflict was managed. A singular residential formation did not emerge from the data. This is not meant to be an exhaustive list of all the possible residential arrangements, but rather highlights how doubled-up residences differ. The possibility exists, for example, that a merged residence with egalitarian decision-making is present in other doubled-up homes or two head of households vie for control in other situations; however, these formations were not present in this study. The differing residential arrangements created differing social environments that influenced how youth participated in the educational process.

Influence of social environments on educational perceptions

Resiliency Theory relies on identifying risk and protective factors influencing outcomes for a specific group. My initial assumption was that living doubled-up created risks to the educational participation of youth. Therefore, resilient youth have access to protective factors that enable them to overcome barriers and achieve educational resilience in spite of living doubled-up. This premise was flawed. Living doubled-up had the potential of increasing both risk and protection.

A brief discussion of the youth's participation in and perceptions of the educational process is warranted before turning to factors influencing educational resilience. Consistent with previous research (Tierney, Gupton & Hallett, 2008), the youth in this study possessed future aspirations requiring some form of post-secondary education. Their goals ranged from training to become a firefighter to attending medical school. Although the youth may not have settled on a singular career goal, the options under consideration required at least completion of high school and earning a professional certification at a trade school or community college. Aspirations connected to both the youth's interests and a desire to achieve residential stability in the future. For example, Kylee hoped to earn enough money to purchase a house for her family and Juan dreamed of owning a BMW—a symbol, in his view, of financial stability.

Their participation in the educational process did not always reflect the desire to graduate from high school and transition to postsecondary education. Three themes emerged that helped explain the discrepancy between future aspirations and daily participation: 1) mobility and perception of stability; 2) division of labor; and 3) factors outside the residence.

Mobility and perceived stability

The participants had varying degrees of residential mobility. Although movement between residences occurred at varying rates, the uncertainty about stability was salient for each of the youth. I begin by discussing residential movement before discussing perceptions of stability.

Residential and school transitions occurred at differing rates. Marco and Juan had relatively stable residential and school contexts whereas Kylee and Isaac experienced higher rates of movement, which resulted in different educational settings each year. Movement between residences disrupted the formation of relationships with peers, educators and mentors. Changing school sites and districts also resulted in a discontinuity of educational services. Kylee, who attended a different school each year, was enrolled in courses at her current school based upon availability, but she did not get academic advising to create a clear path to graduation. Isaac, a naturally shy individual, had a difficult time navigating the social demands of school, which was magnified by the high rate of movement. Marco experienced numerous residential movements over a short period in elementary school, but remained in the same house for nearly a decade. Juan's residential history had the fewest number of movements; however, the most recent change involved moving to a new country. High rates of mobility influenced the stability of their social networks, access to information about the educational process, and classroom experiences.

Increased movement resulted in fragmented social networks. Developing and maintaining peer relationships was challenging for youth who shifted residences and schools frequently. Kylee and Isaac were frustrated by the cycle of creating and dissolving relationships each time they moved, but responded differently to disruption in their social networks. Movement between school sites limited their ability to create a close bond with teachers, counselors and mentors who could guide them through the educational process and provide information about transitioning to postsecondary institutions. Whereas Juan and Marco established relationships with educational mentors over the course of their high school career, Kylee and Isaac had to reestablish these connections each time they enrolled at a new school. Kylee explained that she was generally more interested in navigating the social environment before building relationships with teachers and Isaac did not expect to receive support from school staff. After a while Isaac became uncomfortable with the school environment and felt a sense of shame around peers who engaged in the educational process.

Classroom instruction, although not the primary focus of this study, was influenced by mobility. Kylee mentioned being placed in classes based upon availability and had difficulty changing curriculum in the middle of the school year. Both Isaac and Kylee had periods ranging from a month to a year when they did not attend school during or after a residential transition. These findings were consistent with previous research with other groups of mobile student populations (Buckner, 2001; Corwin, 2008; Rafferty & Rollins, 1989).

Actual movement was a reality for two of the participants, but a fear of instability permeated all of the youth's lives. For Kylee and Isaac, residential instability was undesirable, but expected. The experience was different for Juan and Marco who had relatively stable residential histories; however, uncertainty about future instability was salient to varying degrees. Juan's family lived in the same apartment for nearly three years, but meeting monthly financial obligations was a challenge. During the final few months of this study his mother lost one of her jobs and his grandfather became unemployed. His grandfather's son moved into the apartment, but finding employment proved to be a challenge because of his undocumented status and limited English proficiency. Juan started working 22 hours a week to help pay the bills. He was uncertain how long his family would be able to afford living in the apartment. For Marco the situation differed. His aunt owned the home where he lived with his father and sister. His family's residential stability was contingent upon following his aunt's rules. The instability of the residence became a reality when his sister was "evicted" from the house.

Movement also occurred within residences. The number of households and their composition changed, at times with little notice, throughout the seven-month period of this study. Isaac's residence exemplified this. The number of people in the residence ranged from 5 to 13. At the beginning of the study, four households lived together, but it dwindled down to two during the final month and created an economic crisis for the remaining households. The composition of Juan's residence shifted several times during the three years since he moved to Los Angeles. Each adjustment in households required renegotiating space and financial obligations. Whether or not movement occurred, uncertainty about residential stability was an aspect of the youth's social environment.

Division of labor

Shared households and merged residences approached childrearing in different ways. Parents in shared residences were responsible for their children's discipline and education in addition to managing other aspects of the home. In Juan's situation, his mother worked two jobs and had little energy to devote to her children. He took responsibility for his younger siblings' behavior and educational participation. His mother had a general sense of Juan's schooling, but did not assist with the process of applying to college and was unable to attend his school functions. Isaac's stepmother did not work, but devoted her energy to meeting the basic needs of the residence. Managing the minimal resources she received from welfare and dealing with disgruntled landlords took the majority of her time. In both of these residences, parents wanted their children to achieve educational success; however, meeting basic needs and household responsibilities took precedence.

Merged households allowed parents to specialize. The adult in the residence who took responsibility for school attendance and completion of homework was not always the biological parent. Kylee's mother was responsible for ensuring that all of the children—her biological children and those of her roommate—were fed and attended school. Marco's aunt monitored the educational participation of her children as well as her niece and nephew. Even though Marco missed school on occasion, his behavior was monitored to ensure that his attendance did not negatively impact his educational progress. His oldest cousin, Aaron, provided guidance concerning postsecondary education for the entire residence. In both cases, the biological parent was aware of their children's educational progress, but the daily monitoring was delegated to one person within the residence. The perceived family bonds within these residences were stronger than the households that kept responsibility for childrearing separate.

The structure of the residence (i.e. merged verses shared) influenced the amount of time parents had to devote to the educational process. Merged households had the potential to serve as a protective factor. The specialization of tasks enabled one parent to take responsibility for school attendance, homework completion, and encouraging educational success for all children in the residence. The other parent focused on managing the financial aspects of the home. Merged households also pooled resources, which enabled them to have access to computers, internet and space to complete homework. On the other hand, shared residences became a risk to educational success. Parents were overwhelmed by the responsibility of meeting the basic needs of their children and managing the increased level of conflict between households. I am not suggesting that these parents did not care about their children's educational success, but rather other aspects of caring for their children took the majority of their time and energy. Structure of the residence influenced the youth's educational participation, but did not determine either success or failure. As noted in Chapter 2, the accumulation of factors better explains educational resilience than a single factor. Specifically, the relationship between the social network within and outside of the home shaped how youth perceived the educational process.

Factors outside the residence

The focus of this study was the residential context of youth living doubled-up; however, factors outside the home influenced how participants responded to the residential context and, conversely, the residential context influenced how youth responded to outside factors. Gang violence, exposure to drugs and alcohol, and mentoring programs were relevant to the educational resilience of youth in this study. I briefly discuss factors outside the home that helped shape their perception of education.

All the youth lived in low-income neighborhoods plagued by gang violence. Isaac was the only participant with direct gang connections; however, the other youth discussed the influence gang activity had on their lives. For example, Juan avoided specific streets and individuals connected with gangs. During the final month of the school year, two youth were shot in the neighborhood where Isaac, Kylee and Marco lived. The first was a female in middle school who was shot in front of the apartment complex where Kylee lived and the other was a male walking into the high school Marco attended. Police reports published in the newspaper connected both of these assaults to gang affiliations. The youth and members of their residence discussed how violence in the neighborhood forced them to spend the majority of their time inside their homes. Inability to utilize space outside the residence magnified the limited space. In particular, youth with elementary-aged siblings and roommates complained that younger residents got bored playing inside.

Participants were exposed to, and at times participated in, substance use. With the exception of Juan, youth identified at least one adult in the home who regularly used drugs or alcohol. The participants' personal use ranged from abstinence to experimentation to frequent use. Juan and Kylee feared that engaging in substance use may lead to addiction or other health disorders. Marco drank alcohol when his cousins hosted a party or occasionally with friends on the weekends. Isaac consumed alcohol and drugs on a daily basis, which limited his ability and motivation to engage in the educational process.

In addition to risks posed by gang violence and substance use, participants discussed mentoring relationships that varied in form and purpose. Kylee attended a mentoring group designed to empower females in high school by establishing relationships with women in professional careers. However, Kylee enrolled in the group to fulfill her required service hours for graduation and did not actively engage in the process. Isaac's mentor, who worked for a social service agency, primarily assisted with meeting basic needs and providing emotional support. Once a month he would take Isaac to dinner and discuss issues that may have arisen between visits. Typically the conversations dealt with resources that the family was unable to access (e.g. food and rent). His mentor encouraged Isaac to enroll in school, but took few steps to assist with the process or enforce consequences for dropping out. Marco and Juan had mentors who intentionally focused on navigating high school and transitioning to a university. Marco's cousins, who successfully navigated this transition, encouraged him to attend school and assisted with the application process for colleges, scholarships and financial aid. He also enrolled in a college preparation course at his high school with a teacher who provided additional guidance. Juan had teachers who provided support; however, the most influential relationship developed when he enrolled in a mentoring program at a local university. The mentor he was assigned met with him a few times each month as well as regularly corresponding via email and telephone. The relationship focused on applications for financial aid and scholarships as well as preparing for the transition to college.

Factors outside the youth's residences influenced their educational resilience. In the section that follows, I discuss specific aspects of the residential context that influenced the youth's participation in the educational process. I then turn to the relationship between factors present within the residence and support provided by the social network.

Risk and protection of residential structure

Living doubled-up had general risk and protective qualities. Space was limited. Families relied on the financial stability of other households, which meant that the entire residence faced loss of shelter if one of the residences fell into a crisis or a conflict disrupted the ability of households to live together. However, sharing economic responsibilities with multiple households enabled families to achieve a higher standard of living than they may have been able to independently. Although this residential formation was crowded, the youth had more space and privacy than they may have had living in a shelter, hotel, single room occupancy or vehicle. These qualities were shared by all participants; however, aspects of protection and risk differed depending upon the structure of the residence. The two aforementioned residential formations—separate households and merged residences—influenced educational resilience in distinct ways.

Separate households as a risk factor

Living with multiple households in a single residence posed risks to the educational resilience of youth in separate households. The structure of relationships between households resulted in limited collaboration and conflict. Both of these influenced the youth's educational participation. Separate households split monthly utility bills and management of the home was divided. Each parent took responsibility for his or her own children, which included ensuring children attended school with homework completed and in proper uniform. In addition, these parents managed the money remaining after paying rent and utilities to purchase food, necessities and entertainment for their families individually. The lack of collaboration created more overall work.

Living adjacent without collaboration meant that each parent had to take responsibility for childrearing individually. In addition to dealing with the stress of making ends meet, parents had to make choices about how much time to devote to meeting his or her children's basic needs, supporting their educational participation, and managing their behavior. For both Isaac and Juan, meeting basic needs drained the majority of their parents' time and money. Both of their parents expressed the desire for their children to be successful in school, but they had little time or energy to dedicate to the educational needs of their children.

These residences benefited from shared financial responsibilities, but limited collaboration resulted in conflict between households. Disagreements arose concerning the allocation of space and distribution of resources between families. Since households did not function as a single unit, often the assumption was that one household benefited and the other lost. Mounting tension built between households because conflict was not necessarily resolved. Economic necessity kept households in the same residence; however, each family was willing to consider alternative living arrangements.

The individuals living within these residences changed frequently. The bond between households was not strong; therefore, a household may leave with little notice if a more appealing opportunity arose and the remaining households would then struggle to make up for the economic loss. Space and financial responsibilities were renegotiated each time individuals entered or exited the residence. As mentioned earlier, the heightened level of conflict already present in these homes magnified the difficulty of adding new households.

Merged households as a protective factor

Merging households into a unified residence had a protective influence on the youth's educational resilience. Through collaboration, these families were able to manage conflict and divide responsibilities between parents. This residential formation also increased the level of emotional and financial interconnectedness of the residents.

Merged residences reduced the level of conflict by functioning as a single unit with shared interests and assigning a head of household. The level of competition between households decreased as collaboration increased. Kylee's residence shared space and resources. Groceries, bills, entertainment, vehicles, clothes and school supplies were purchased together. In preparation for Monique's birthday party, Lucy purchased a new outfit for all of the children. Although Monique was not her biological child, she took responsibility for planning the party and decorating the home of Angela's mother. Families shared meals and had a clear system to complete household tasks. The competition between households decreased because resources and space were communal. When conflict arose that individuals were unable to resolve in a merged home, the head of the household made a decision.

Parents divided household responsibilities allowing each to specialize in the merged residences. Instead of each household preparing meals, assisting children with homework, working outside the home, and providing childcare, these responsibilities were divided between the parents. In Kylee's case, Angela worked two fulltime jobs while Lucy took responsibility for raising the children and managing the home. All three of the parents in Marco's home worked; however, his aunt took the added responsibility of preparing meals and childrearing. The two men, his father and uncle, maintained the physical appearance of the home (e.g. yard work and home repairs). Although not the focus of this study, it is worth noting that both of the merged residences formed a situation where traditional gender roles were assumed. Even in Kylee's residence with two female parents,

Angela became the "man of the family" and Lucy, presumably, assumed stereo-typically female roles. Through the specialization of responsibilities, tasks were completed more effectively and efficiently. The shared responsibility enabled youth to get more frequent supervision and educational support.

Families in merged residences were interconnected emotionally and financially. Through raising children together, the parents had a shared investment in the educational success of all children. Purchasing items together created long-term financial connections that were reinforced by contractual obligations. The car Lucy and Angela purchased together required the women to consider their relationship years in advance. Interconnectedness provided an added level of stability. The families had stronger financial and emotional bonds that made exiting the residence more difficult than for those living in separate households.

Doubled-up youth and educational resilience

The findings from this study contribute to Resiliency Theory—and educational resilience in particular—in at least three ways. First, the presence of a risk or protective factor alone did not relate to a specific outcome. *How* the participant experienced the factor shaped the youth's response. This confirms the idea that resilience should be viewed as a process and not a stagnant trait (Luthar & Cicchetti, 2000). Most studies identify lists and do not actually explore how these factors occur or change over time. Quantitative studies are helpful for identifying how factors correlate at the population level; however, additional research is warranted that focuses on how individuals experience risk and protection.

Second, this study builds upon previous work that argues that subgroups of homeless youth experience the educational process differently (Finley & Finley, 1999; Tierney, Gupton & Hallett, 2008; Smith & Ferrari, 1997). Previous studies of homeless youth have looked at the risks associated with living on the streets or in shelters. Youth living doubled-up were influenced by risk factors similar to other subgroups of homeless youth, including exposure to substance abuse, neighborhoods plagued by gang violence, unstable living environments, and shame associated with their living conditions (Ensign & Santelli, 1998; Lifson & Halcon, 2001; Rew, Taylor-Seehafer & Fitzgerald, 2001; Thompson, Zittel-Palamara & Maccio, 2004). However, the influence these factors had on the youth appeared to be less pervasive than experienced by youth on the streets and in shelters. The residential situations of the youth on the streets and in shelters are unstable, whereas I consider the living arrangements in doubled-up households as semi-stable. Previous studies have also found that homeless individuals living on the streets or in shelters developed social support systems with others in similar situations (Bender *et al.*, 2007; Duneier, 1999; Liebow, 1993). Doubled-up youth did not possess the same level of inter-connectedness with others in the same residential environment. The relationships formed within the residence were important, but the youth did not intentionally establish connections and emotional support systems with others living doubled-up.

Similar to other subgroups of homeless, youth living doubled-up were exposed to drugs, alcohol and violence. The design of this study limited my ability to assert if the level of involvement in these acts was at the same level as other youth. I focused primarily on how this residential situation was similar to and different from other subgroups of homeless youth.

Finally, the residential formation alone was not deterministic. Other factors in the lives of the youth worked together to influence resilience. Table 8.2 illustrates how the residential formation and social network outside the home shaped educational resilience. Being doubled-up did not predestine a youth to either educational success or failure. However, the residential structure could increase either risk or protection. Residential structure is only one aspect of the youth's resilience. Consistent with previous research, many factors influenced the educational resilience, including friends, substance use, mentor relationships, educational background of family, and relationships with educators (Eckert, 1989; Fordham, 1996; Stanton-Salazar, 1997, 2001; Willis, 1977).

The youth in this study illustrate how the interaction between factors may influence how a youth develops educational resilience. I explored the relationship between residential structure and social network factors outside of the home. Living in a merged residence with an adult who encouraged educational participation coupled with a social network outside the home that provided information about the educational process created the most protective environment for youth. On the other hand, living in a separate residence without an adult who monitored

TABLE 8.2 Doubled-up youth and educational resilience

	Merged residence	Separate households
Outside support	The residential structure and social network work in unison to support the youth's educational resilience	The social network outside the home provides educational support that may be lacking within the home. Educational resilience is possible if the youth's social network accommodates for the conflict and limited guidance from within the residence
Limited outside support	The residential structure encourages educational participation that may be lacking in the youth's social network outside the home. If the network within the home has access to resources the student may achieve educational resilience	The limited structure within the home and deviant social peer network work in conjunction to discourage educational resilience

educational participation coupled with an absence of social network support outside of the home was the least supportive. The youth with either a supportive residential environment or social network were able to develop educational resilience if they received both information about the educational process and encouragement to participate in school. Before turning to the implications of these findings, I review how each of the youth experienced educational resilience.

Marco lived in a merged residence with outside support. Protective qualities of both his residence and social network encouraged his engagement in the educational process. His family expected Marco to attend school on a regular basis, pass classes, and transition into college. He developed relationships with a teacher who provided access to information about applying to a postsecondary institution and received guidance from his cousin regarding the financial aid process. Although he did not have a high level of intrinsic motivation, support within and outside his residence enabled him to achieve educational resilience.

Kylee lived in a merged residence with limited outside support. Expectations within the household encouraged her participation in high school. The living arrangement had protective qualities; however, Kylee was not educationally resilient. Her mother wanted her children to be successful, but had limited knowledge of the educational process. Kylee's network of peers and adults was unable to provide her with the guidance necessary to complete high school within the four-year period and adequately prepare for the transition to postsecondary education. The arrangement supported attendance, not necessarily achievement.

Juan lived in a separate household with outside support. The structure of his residence created conflict between families and limited his access to educational support. In addition, he took on additional responsibility for childrearing and assisting with financially supporting the residence. Juan's peer and adult network outside the residence encouraged his educational participation and provided him with guidance as he transitioned to postsecondary education. In his situation, the residential structure was a risk factor, but other protective qualities in his life allowed him to achieve educational resilience.

Isaac lived in a separate household without outside support. The chaotic residential environment was not conducive to educational support. The crowded living environment encouraged his stepmother and other residents to focus attention on meeting basic needs. No one within the residence had graduated from high school or understood how to transition to postsecondary education. His lack of engagement went unnoticed. Isaac's peer network outside the home further distanced him from the educational process as he was encouraged to participate in gangs, use drugs and alcohol, and drop out of school. Although Isaac had aspirations, the residential structure coupled with risks outside the home discouraged his educational resilience.

The youth in this study illustrate the relationship between residential structure and social network factors outside of the home. Living in a merged residence with an adult who encouraged educational participation coupled with a social network outside the home that provided information about the educational process created the most protective environment for youth. On the other hand, living in a separate residence without an adult who monitored educational participation coupled with an absence of social network support outside of the home was the least supportive. The youth with either a supportive residential environment or social network were able to develop educational resilience if they received both information about the educational process and encouragement to participate in school.

Living in a doubled-up residence did not result in a singular experience. There was the potential to have both positive and negative influences. This exploratory study begins the discussion about diversity within this subcategory of homelessness, but further study is warranted to test the accuracy and identify other residential formations. In the chapter that follows, I present a few recommendations for policy and practice based upon the findings.

9

IMPLICATIONS FOR POLICY AND PRACTICE

The current study provides guidance for developing programs and policies that support students without residential stability. Given that this living arrangement can increase both protection and risk, programs and services need to be carefully designed to support residences struggling without disrupting those functioning successfully. The experiences of the youth and families reinforce previous studies that have found that living doubled-up is part of the cycle of homelessness. While Isaac's family used this residential arrangement to move out of a welfare hotel, the other families lived doubled-up to avoid seeking refuge in a homeless shelter or a similarly unstable environment. All families lived on the brink of economic and residential crisis. Reducing the size of the homeless population requires assisting those individuals without residential stability to secure a home as well as preventing additional individuals who may be struggling in semi-stable environment. Unfortunately, families on the verge of economic crisis do not always get the same level of attention or support as those already on the streets or in shelters.

Developing programming and policies for doubled-up families has the potential to both assist those transitioning out of homelessness as well as reducing the number who slip into residential instability. In particular, I focus on how the residential environment can be supported to encourage educational participation. All the youth in this study viewed education as a path toward a more stable future; however, not all of them had access to information and supportive relationships that could make their dreams a reality. A few lessons can be learned from the families who shared their lives and stories. Three aspects warrant discussion: reconsidering the terms used to define this population, focusing on supporting households without a deficit perspective, and identifying ways to increase access to postsecondary education.

Reconsidering terms

The federal law protecting educational access of youth living doubled-up categorizes them under the larger umbrella of *homeless*. This inclusive term represents youth living in a variety of unstable environments, including in cars, shelters, motels, and doubled-up residences. Programs funded by this law generally are identified as homeless programs. For example, each school district is required to identify a homeless liaison responsible for implementing federal mandates and distributing resources. State and district posters and brochures describing the law typically explain services available for homeless students. These services include assistance purchasing backpacks and supplies, the ability to remain at a school site until the end of a school year even if the student moves, and access support services provided by the district homeless liaison. A few scholarships and financial aid provisions also exist for homeless students pursuing a postsecondary degree. The utility of these programs depends upon the terms used to promote and recruit. Since doubled-up youth live in a space between housed and homeless, the experiences of the families in this book provide an opportunity to reconceptualize *home*. After doing so, I discuss how using the term homeless can have unintended exclusionary consequences.

The youth did not view themselves as homeless. This was especially true for youth who had experienced other forms of residential instability (i.e. welfare hotel or living on the streets). All of the youth identified their house or apartment as home. Therefore, how could they be homeless? Granted, all of the youth aspired to move into a single family residence and eventually purchase a home of their own. They clearly ascribed to the American Dream of a stable income and homeownership. Living in a doubled-up residence may not have been ideal, but categorizing their residential situation with those living in shelters or on the street was confusing and offensive.

Provisions like McKinney–Vento are intended to assist youth experiencing residential instability. These laws are created with the best intentions by policymakers coming from a middle- or upper-class perspective. Four families living in a small apartment does not fit their definition of home. Therefore, policies have been created to assist students perceived as homeless. Grouping doubled-up youth under the umbrella of homelessness has led to avoidance, resentment and shame. These families want assistance getting a house without shaming their current home. Every child needs to feel safe and validated in their home. Sending a message that they do not actually have a home can lead to insecurity. Policies designed to support families in securing stable housing while valuing where the students already feel at home will have more success.

I am not arguing that the youth and families presented here would not benefit from the protections provided by McKinney–Vento. In particular, youth living in separate households experienced increased conflict that could result in a high level of residential mobility. Living on the verge of economic crisis meant that support with backpacks and supplies could make the difference between attending school or not. However, the policy reinforces the value placed on individualism. The unintended message youth living doubled-up hear is that their families have not achieved the ideal standard. Policies at the federal level require categorization to distribute resources. I appreciate why federal mandates group all youth under one categorization. However, programs at the ground level may need to reconsider language.

Words matter. The youth in this study did not identify with the term *homeless*. Participants did not contact the homeless liaison or pick up brochures explaining rights protected by McKinney–Vento. Unlike other subgroups of youth that rejected the classification of homelessness, these youth and families were unaware that their residential situation was part of the discussion. Putting theoretical considerations aside, using the term homeless to describe programs and services discouraged doubled-up youth and families from seeking support. For example, few high school students would want to have it announced that they received a scholarship for homeless youth or attended a seminar designed to assist families out of homelessness. Even if federal funding is allocated for homeless youth, the actual programs may consider different terminology.

If, as the federal government has determined, these youth warrant the protections outlined in McKinney–Vento, new terms need to be used to attract the attention of those who the law is designed to support. *Highly mobile* is one possibility; however, actual physical mobility may not occur. Youth may live in the same doubled-up residence, shelter, or hotel for years at a time. Although these environments could be semi-stable and warrant additional support, youth and families may not self-identify as being highly mobile. Another possibility is to avoid the word homeless and use subcategories (e.g. youth living in a shelter and doubled-up families) for promotional purposes. This approach would enable states and districts to distinguish how aspects of the federal law may be used to support each subpopulation. In addition, youth and families may be more likely to self-identify as belonging to one of these subcategories. Using terms like "doubled-up" or "shared residence" may be more conducive for self-identification and increase the likelihood of identifying families in need of assistance.

Supporting households

Findings suggest that merged residences allow families to collaborate more effectively, which encourages educational participation. Further study with families living doubled-up is warranted to determine the range of household arrangements as well as the connection between residential formations and educational resilience. Based on the current study, a few aspects of how educational institutions interact with these youth deserve consideration.

Interactions with parents

The person responsible for the education of youth in a residence may not be the biological parent. Complex living environments may require delegation of tasks in order to maintain a functional, semi-stable residence. The primary person responsible for ensuring youth complete homework and attend school could be a sibling, aunt, grandparent or roommate. I am not suggesting that rights or responsibilities of the biological parent be diminished, but rather acknowledge that living arrangements shape how residences view family and delegate responsibility. The limited presence of biological parents at the school site does not necessarily mean that they do not care about the educational success of their children. Schools and educational programs, with the biological parent's permission, should be open to working collaboratively with whoever has been identified as the primary person responsible for the student's educational outcomes.

This requires developing of a relationship with students and families. McKinney–Vento requires that school districts identify a homeless liaison responsible for ensuring compliance with federal mandates and supporting families experiencing residential instability. Large urban districts like Los Angeles have found that one person cannot adequately identify and assist all of the youth covered by the mandate. Therefore, they require a staff member at each school site be identified who works with the district homeless liaison. Unfortunately, budget shortages impede schools' ability to hire a person designated for this task; the responsibility is added to a counselor or administrator who may feel overburdened with other responsibilities. Supporting these youth and families requires each school site have a contact person who is aware of the law, can deal with the issue compassionately, and has time to work with families.

Supporting functional residences

Homeless advocates may prefer policies and programs that enable single-occupancy dwellings for families transitioning out of a shelter or other unstable environment. The reality of the economic environment does not make such programs politically or financially viable. Until such a time when enough affordable housing units can be created, families living in alternative arrangements will need support. Living doubled-up may be part of the transition out of homelessness or an attempt to avoid falling into homelessness. As a result, those serving this population must consider how to protect these residences while assisting families attempting to move into a more stable environment.

The structure of relationships within the residence influences educational participation. Programs and services could be designed to assist families in developing arrangements within the household that support educational outcomes. Models of successful residences could be developed to provide guidance for struggling residences. The end goal would not be to penalize families, but rather to share information about alternative residential formations that may ease the level of conflict and encourage educational success of youth.

Increasing social network programs

The relationship between households within a doubled-up residence was but one factor influencing educational resilience. Similar to previous studies in low-income communities (e.g. Stanton–Salazar 1997, 2001), this study demonstrates the importance of networks outside the home. Several programs have emerged that offer educational guidance and mentoring to youth in urban areas. These programs often either provide educational or emotional guidance; rarely are both given equal attention. Mentoring relationships that allow youth to form a bond with an adult mentor have the potential to alleviate emotional stress that could lead to involvement in high-risk behavior. These relationships may give youth opportunities to access life outside their community (e.g. museums, plays, and sporting events). These mentoring programs may allow youth to be emotionally available to participate in school and mentors often serve as inspiration.

Providing access to life outside the youth's neighborhood is only one aspect of mentoring that shapes resilience. Programs intentionally designed to guide youth through the educational process have the potential of providing information to students necessary to realize their aspirations. The youth in this study without access to guidance concerning the educational process and transition to postsecondary education had a difficult time taking steps towards reaching their aspirations. Navigating the transition from high school to higher education requires numerous considerations including locating an institution, choosing a major, applying for scholarships and grants, and securing housing. Mentors knowledgeable about the process can guide and encourage students as they move through the process.

Creating postsecondary opportunities

The majority of provisions for youth without residential stability address access to kindergarten through high school graduation. Continued work is necessary to increase access to school as well as encouraging the success of these youth once they arrive at the school site. These youth also need support transitioning to postsecondary education.

A few provisions exist that assist in the transition. For example, high school students can work with the district liaison to get a waiver that allows for homeless students to claim financial independence when applying for federal financial aid. This provision rarely increases the amount of aid distributed through grants and loans because most families have limited financial resources. However, this may allow students to apply for aid when their families do not have access to financial information necessary to fill out forms and can streamline the process for those living in complex residential situations.

Youth without residential stability may need additional support in order to make the transition from high school to college a reality. Housing is an obvious concern. Community colleges often do not have on-campus options. Four-year institutions may have campus housing, but these units close during holidays, vacations or during periods between semesters. Students may not be able to return to their families' home for several reasons. A financial crisis may have forced the family into a less stable residential arrangement, including a shelter, hotel or car. Their former residence may be full or have new members who do not want the college student to return. Or the student may not have the money needed to pay for travel to where his or her family lives. Students from families without residential stability need support in securing a residence that will enable them to participate in the educational process. These options are only viable if they result in minimal cost to the student.

These students may also need access to counseling services once on campus. Transitioning to a postsecondary environment may involve a dramatic shift for these students. In addition to making psychological counseling available to deal with stress, the students may need access to academic and financial support. The residential and school backgrounds of the youth may not have adequately prepared them for the academic rigor of postsecondary education. Allowing students to struggle on their own may reinforce negative perceptions of self if they do not succeed. In addition, the economic context of their childhood may frame how they experience higher education. Fear of student loans and intimidation as a result of tuition costs may preclude some from pursuing higher education. Those who do arrive on campus may feel torn between participating in college and identify ways to financially assist their family. During periods of economic crisis the student may consider diverting portions of the financial aid package to his or her family or may feel an obligation to work in order to assist in paying family bills. In some situations, a student may feel forced to choose between continuing school while ignoring the needs of his or her family and dropping out in order to move home to assist his or her family. A financial counselor on campus can assist students through weighing these options and may be able to identify other means of support.

Conclusion

The lives of the youth in this study illustrate the complexity of doubled-up residences. Assuming these individuals and their families fit easily into one model misses the differing experiences, resources and risks of their residential formations. Each youth in this study had aspirations to pursue a career after college and acquire residential stability in the future. Residential formations coupled with factors present in their social network influenced their ability to participate in the educational process and take the necessary steps towards realizing those dreams.

Future studies may be designed to identify other residential formations that may exist in doubled-up homes. The possibility exists that alternative arrangements exist beyond what was present in this study. Particular attention should be given to the influence each arrangement has on educational participation and outcomes. In addition, future research could test the consistency of these findings in other contexts, including rural communities and urban areas outside of Los Angeles County.

I met with Juan for the final time a few weeks before high school graduation. His confidence concerning his ability to succeed in college steadily increased throughout his senior year of high school as he had continued educational success and secured financial support for tuition. He was nervous about moving to UCLA, but eagerly anticipated graduating from high school and moving away from home. The opportunity to share a dorm room with one other person will be a luxury for Juan. "[My mentor] has been helping me with getting all the paperwork done and stuff," he smiled, "It should be good."

10

EPILOGUE (18 MONTHS LATER)

The study officially ended in the summer of 2009. I had to redefine my relationships with the participants. I attempted to remain in contact with all of the youth; however, my involvement in their lives has been significantly reduced. I spoke with the participants throughout the study about my experiences looking for a job. I moved to Northern California soon after the conclusion of the study. Relocating to another city provided a logical end to our research relationship. I gradually reduced my visits to their homes from weekly to more sporadically.

I encouraged Juan and Marco to remain in contact with me as they pursued a postsecondary education. Kylee and Isaac were less interested in the educational support I could provide. Our relationship remains more informal. Corresponding via Facebook proved to be the most convenient mode of communication as well as occasionally visiting their homes when I was in Los Angeles. Assuming the participants followed a traditional educational plan (four years of high school before transitioning to college), each of the youth would have been in college by the fall semester of 2010. Below I provide a brief summary of each youth's residential situation and educational progress.

Juan graduated from high school in the spring of 2009. He participated in two summer programs designed to help transition between high school and college. His mother and siblings continue to live in the same apartment with extended family members. After more than 20 years working as a housekeeper, his grandmother retired and began collecting Social Security benefits. Juan went home the summer after his first year, but has decided to find alternative arrangements in the coming years. He hopes to help his mother move into a different apartment in the future.

His mentor continues to play an important role in his life. Juan participated in a summer internship that his mentor helped him find. Each semester Juan meets with his mentor a few times to receive guidance with homework and scholarship essays.

He works at a coffee shop near his college campus to help limit student loan debt. At the end of his second year of college he is $12,000 in debt.

Medical school is no longer a goal. Juan enjoys taking sociology and history courses. So, he changed his major to history with an education minor. He plans to get a teaching credential after completing his undergraduate degree. Juan still intends on returning to his community or a similar low-income community as a teacher.

Marco graduated from high school in the spring of 2009. He enjoyed the summer break by spending time with friends and family. His family helped him move to a state college about two hours from Los Angeles. Marco joined a fraternity soon after arriving on campus. Greek life consumed much of his time and energy during the first year of school. He also began dating.

He continues to be an "average" student. Marco has a 2.7 GPA as an environmental health major. His sister, Sasha, moved back in with his family and has begun taking college classes. Both of his cousins remain in the home. Aaron is looking for a new job after a two-year contract ended and Lewie plans to graduate from college in the summer of 2011.

Halfway through his second year, Marco decided to "take a break" from his fraternity and moved back in with his family. He is frustrated by the limited course offerings as result of budget cuts. Each morning he drives "about an hour or so" to college with a friend. He is planning on transferring to the University of California system; he assumes courses will be available on a more consistent basis.

Kylee finished her junior year in the spring of 2009, but was not on track to graduate the following year. She attended school on a regular basis. Lack of access to a guidance counselor limited her understanding of the educational process. She continued to hope that postsecondary education would be an option.

The residence experienced a crisis that disrupted the relationship between the two families. A fight erupted between the two mothers concerning Lucy's continued marijuana use in the home. As Kylee explained, "It was pure drama." Angela planned to move into a new apartment with her two children. Lucy, who remained unemployed, had few options. She contemplated taking her three children to a homeless shelter. She eventually found another place to stay in Watts for a month before moving to Victorville for a few months and then to Pamona (both are cities near Los Angeles). Kylee began her seventh high school in 2010—an independent study charter school. She still hopes to complete her diploma and transition to a community college.

Isaac has not returned to school. Attending a traditional school did not appeal to him because he was so far behind. The independent study program did not provide enough structure and he had a difficult time doing school work in the house. In addition, none of his friends were engaged in the educational process.

The residence was evicted again in the fall of 2009 and the families moved to a new apartment in South Central Los Angeles. The move required crossing gang boundaries. Isaac was affiliated with, but had not officially joined, the gang in his previous neighborhood. Faith and Sydney lost custody of their children in November of 2009. Child Protective Services determined the children were educationally neglected and the home was not suitable for childrearing. Isaac was left in the home because he was nearing his 18th birthday. Faith informed Isaac that he would need to move out in January after his birthday because the state no longer provided her monthly financial support once he became a legal adult. He stayed with a friend for a few weeks before moving into a hotel on Skid Row. Isaac joined a gang and began selling drugs. He was arrested twice on narcotics charges in the summer and fall of 2010. The first court appearance resulted in probation; the second led to a six-month suspended sentence if he moved into a transitional living unit for drug offenders.

Isaac spends the majority of his time in or near Skid Row. He continues to use and sell drugs while on probation. School is not a part of his life.

BIBLIOGRAPHY

Adams, K. S., & Christenson, S. L. (2000). Trust and the family–school relationship: Examination of parent–teacher differences in elementary and secondary grades. *Journal of School Psychology*, 38, 477–97.

Adelman, C. (2006). *The toolbox revisited: Paths to degree completion for high school through college*. Washington, DC: US Department of Education.

Alva, S. A. (1991). Academically invulnerability among Mexican-American students: The importance of protective resources and appraisals. *Hispanic Journal of Behavioral Sciences*, 13(1), 18–34.

Anooshian, L. J. (2005). Violence and aggression in the lives of homeless children: A review. *Aggression and Violent Behavior*, 10(2), 129–52.

Anthony, E. J. (1987). Risk, vulnerability, and resilience: An overview. In E. J. Anthony & B. Cohler (Eds.), *The invulnerable child* (pp. 3–48). New York: Guilford Press.

Ascher, C., & Phenix, D. (2006). *Delivering educational services to homeless youth: The challenges and successes of New York state LEA liaisons*. New York: Institute for Education and Social Policy.

Bartelt, D. (1994). On resilience: Questions of validity. In M. Wang & E. Gordon (Eds.), *Educational resilience in inner-city America* (pp. 97–108). Hillsdale, NJ: Erlbaum.

Bassuk, E. L., Buckner, J. C., Weinreb, L. F., Browne, A., Bassuk, S. S., Dawson, R., et al. (1997). Homeless in female-headed families: Childhood and adult risk and protective factors. *American Journal of Public Health*, 87(2), 241–48.

Bender, K., Thompson, S. J., McManus, H., Lantry, J., Flynn, P. M. (2007). Capacity of survival: Exploring strengths of homeless street youth. *Child and Youth Care Forum*, 36(1), 25–42.

Berliner, B., Barrat, V. X., Fong, A. B., & Shirk, P. B. (2008). *Reenrollment of high school dropouts in a large, urban school district* (Issues & Answers Report, REL 2008–No. 056). Washington, DC: US Department of Education, Institute of Education Sciences, National Center for Education Evaluation and Regional Assistance, Regional Educational Laboratory West.

Berndt, T. (1990). *Relations of friendships and peer acceptance to adolescents' self-evaluations*. Paper presented at the Annual Meeting of the American Educational Research Association, Boston, MA.

Birch, H. G., & Gussow, J. D. (1970). *Disadvantaged children: Health, nutrition, and school failure*. New York: Harcourt, Brace & World.

Bolland, J. M., & McCallum, D. M. (2002). Touched by homelessness: An examination of hospitality for the down and out. *Research and Practice*, 92(1), 116–18.

Bring Los Angeles Home (2004). *Homelessness in Los Angeles: A summary of recent research.* Los Angeles: Institute for the Study of Homelessness and Poverty.

Buckner, J. C. (2001). Predictors of academic achievement among homeless and low-income housed children. *Journal of School Psychology*, 39(1), 45–69.

Buckner, J. C., Mezzacappa, E., & Beardslee, W. R. (2003). Characteristics of resilient youths living in poverty: The role of self-regulatory processes. *Development and Psychopathology*, 15, 139–62.

Cauce, A. M., Hiraga, Y., Graves, D., Gonzales, N., Ryan-Finn, K., & Grove, K. (1996). African American mothers and their adolescent daughters: Closeness, conflict, and control. In B. J. Leadbeater & N. Ways (Eds.), *Urban girls: Resisting stereotypes, creating identities* (pp. 100–16). New York: New York University Press.

Cauce, A. M., Stewart, A., Rodriguez, M. D., Cochran, B., & Ginzler, J. (2003). Overcoming the odds? Adolescent development in the context of urban poverty. In S. S. Luthar (Ed.), *Resilience and vulnerability: Adaptation in the context of childhood adversities* (pp. 343–63). New York: Cambridge University Press.

Christiansen, E. J., & Evans, W. P. (2005). Adolescent victimization: Testing models of resiliency by gender. *The Journal of Early Adolescence*, 25, 298–316.

Cicchetti, D., Ackerman, B. P., & Izard, C. E. (1995). Emotions and emotion regulation in developmental psychology. *Development and Psychopathology*, 7, 1–10.

Cicchetti, D., & Lynch, M. (1993). Toward an ecological/transactional model of community violence and child maltreatment: Consequences for children's development. *Psychiatry*, 56, 96–118.

Corwin, Z. B. (2008). *College, connections and care: How mobility and social capital affect college preparation for youth in foster care.* Los Angeles, CA: University of Southern California.

Corwin, Z. B., Venegas, K. M., Oliverez, P. M., & Colyar, J. E. (2004). School counsel: How appropriate guidance affects college going. *Urban Education*, 39(4), 442–57.

Costello, E. J., & Angold, A. (2000). Developmental epidemiology: A framework for developmental psychopathology. In A. Sameroff, M. Lewis, & S. Miller (Eds.), *Handbook of developmental psychopathology* (pp. 57–73). New York: Plenum.

Cowen, E. L., & Work, W. C. (1988). Resilient children, psychological wellness, and primary prevention. *American Journal of Community Psychology*, 16, 591–607.

Creswell, J. W. (2007). *Qualitative inquiry and research design: Choosing among five traditions, second edition.* Thousand Oaks, CA: Sage.

Culhane, J. F., Webb, D., Grim, S., Metraux, S., & Culhane, D. (2003). Prevalence of child welfare services involvement among homeless and low-income mothers: A five-year birth cohort study. *Journal of Sociology and Social Welfare*, 30(3), 79–95.

Deater-Deckard, K., Ivy, L., & Smith, J. (2005). Resilience in gene-environment transactions. In I. Goldstein & R. B. Brooks (Eds.), *Handbook of resilience in children* (pp. 49–64). New York: Kluwer Academic/Plenum.

Decter, A. (2007). *Lost in the shuffle: The impact of homelessness on children's education in Toronto.* Toronto, Ontario: Community Social Planning Council of Toronto.

Dekovic, M. (1999). Risk and protective factors in the development of problem behavior during adolescence. *Journal of Youth and Adolescence*, 28(6), 667–85.

Dougherty, C., Millor, L., & Jian, S. (2006). *The relationship between Advanced Placement and college graduation: 2005 AP Study Series.* Austin, TX: National Center for Educational Accountability.

Dounay, J. (2006). *Ensuring rigor in the high school curriculum: What states are doing.* Denver, CO: Education Commission to the States.

Duneier, M. (1999). *Sidewalk.* New York: Farrar, Straus, & Giroux.

Durlak, J. A. (1998). Common risk and protective factors in successful prevention programs. *American Journal of Orthopsychiatry*, 68(4), 512–20.

Dyrness, G. R., Spoto, P., & Thompson, M. (2003). *Crisis on the streets: Homeless women and children in Los Angeles*. Los Angeles, CA: University of Southern California Center for Religion and Civic Culture.

Eckert, P. (1989). *Jocks and burnouts: Social categories and identity in the high school*. New York: Teachers College Press.

Edwards, J. M., Iritani, B. J., & Hallfors, D. D. (2006). Prevalence and correlates of exchanging sex for drugs or money among adolescents in the United States. *Sexually Transmitted Infections*, 82(5), 354–58.

Ensign, J., & Santelli, J. (1998). Health status and service use: Comparison of adolescents at a school-based health clinic with homeless adolescents. *Archives of Pediatrics and Adolescent Medicine*, 152(1), 20–24.

Epstein, I. (1996). Educating street children: Some cross-cultural perspectives. *Comparative Education*, 32(3), 289–302.

Erlenbusch, B., O'Conner, K., Downing, S., & Phillips, S. W. (2008). *Foreclosure to homelessness: The forgotten victims of the subprime crisis*. Washington, DC: National Coalition for the Homeless.

Eyrich-Garg, K. M., Cacciola, J. S., Carise, D., Lynch, K. G., & McLellan, A. T. (2008). Individual characteristics of the literally homeless, marginally housed, and impoverished in a US substance abuse treatment-seeking sample. *Social Psychiatry and Psychiatric Epidemiology*, 43(10), 831–42.

Felner, R. D. (2005). Poverty in childhood and adolescence. In I. Goldstein & R. B. Brooks (Eds.), *Handbook of resilience in children* (pp. 125–48). New York: Kluwer Academic/Plenum.

Felner, R. D., Silverman, M. M., & Felner, T. Y. (2000). Primary prevention: Conceptual and methodological issues in the development of science of prevention in mental health and social intervention. In J. Rappaport & E. Seidman (Eds.), *Handbook of community psychology* (pp. 9–42). New York: Kluwer Academic/Plenum.

Fergus, S., & Zimmerman, M. A. (2005). Adolescent resilience: A framework for understanding healthy development in the face of risk. *Annual Review of Public Health*, 26, 399–419.

Ferguson, K. M. (2009). Exploring family environment characteristics and multiple abuse experiences among homeless youth. *Journal of Interpersonal Violence*, 24(1), 1875–91.

Ferguson, K. M., Jun, J., Bender, K., Thompson, S., & Pollio, D. (2010). A comparison of addiction and transience among street youth: Los Angeles, California, Austin, Texas, and St. Louis, Missouri. *Community Mental Health Journal*, 46(3), 296–307.

Fergusson, D. M., & Horwood, L. J. (2003). Resilience to childhood adversity: Results of a 21-year study. In S. S. Luthar (Ed.), *Resilience and vulnerability: Adaptation in the context of childhood adversities* (pp. 130–55). New York: Cambridge University Press.

Fernandes, A. L. (2007). *Runaway and homeless youth: Demographics, programs, and emerging issues*. Washington, DC: Congressional Research Service.

Finley, S., & Finley, M. (1999). Sp'ange: A research story. *Qualitative Inquiry*, 5(3), 313–37.

Flaming, D., & Tepper, P. (2004). *Ten-year strategy to end homelessness: Public discussion draft*. Prepared by the Partnership to End Homelessness.

Fordham, S. (1996). *Blacked out: Dilemmas of race, identity, and success at Capital High*. Chicago: University of Chicago Press.

Freeman, L., & Hamilton, D. (2008). *A count of homeless youth in New York City*. New York: Empire State Coalition of Youth and Family Services.

Garbarino, J. (2001). Making sense of senseless youth violence. In J. M. Richman & M. W. Fraser (Eds.), *The context of youth violence: Resilience, risk and protection* (pp. 83–96). Westport, CT: Praeger.

Gardner, C., & Troupe, Q. (2006). *The pursuit of happyness*. New York: HarperCollins.

Garmezy, N. (1985). Stress-resistant children: The search for protective factors. In J. E. Stevenson (Ed.), *Recent research in developmental psychopathology (Journal of Child Psychology and Psychiatry* Book Suppl. No. 4, pp. 213–33). Oxford: Pergamon.

—— (1991). Resilience and vulnerability to adverse development outcomes associated with poverty. *American Behavioral Scientist, 34,* 416–30.

Gayles, J. (2005). Playing the game and paying the price: Academic resilience among three high-achieving African American males. *Anthropology and Education Quarterly,* 36(3), 250–64.

Glantz, M. D., & Johnson, J. L. (1999). *Resilience and development: Positive life adaptations—longitudinal research in the social and behavior sciences.* New York: Kluwer Academic/Plenum.

Gonzalez, R., & Padilla, A. M. (1997). The academic resilience of Mexican American high school students. *Hispanic Journal of Behavioral Sciences,* 19(3), 301–17.

Greene, J. M., Ennett, S. T., & Ringwalt, C. L. (1999). Prevalence and correlates of survival sex among runaway and homeless youth. *American Journal of Public Health,* 89(9), 1406–9.

Greene, J. M., & Ringwalt, C. L. (1998). Pregnancy among three national samples of runaway and homeless youth. *Journal of Adolescent Health,* 23(6), 370–77.

Halcon, L. L., & Lifson, A. R. (2004). Prevalence and predictors of sexual risks among homeless youth. *Journal of Youth and Adolescence,* 33(1), 71–80.

Hallett, R. E. (2010). Homeless: How residential instability complicates students' lives. *About Campus,* 15(3), 11–16.

—— (forthcoming). Living doubled-up: Diverse environments and educational outcomes. *Education & Urban Society.*

Hallett, R. E., & Venegas, K. M. (2011). Is increased access enough? Advanced Placement courses, quality, and success in low-income urban schools. *Journal for the Education of the Gifted,* 34(3), 468–87.

Hammersley, M. (1992). *What's wrong with ethnography?* New York: Routledge.

Holme, J. J. (2002). Buying homes, buying schools: School choice and the social construction of school quality. *Harvard Educational Review,* 72(2), 177–205.

Jackson, S., & Martin, P. Y. (1998). Surviving the care system: Education and resilience. *Journal of Adolescence,* 21, 569–83.

Jaffee, S. R. (2005). Family violence and parent psychopathology: Implications for children's socioemotional development and resilience. In I. Goldstein & R. B. Brooks (Eds.), *Handbook of resilience in children* (pp. 149–63). New York: Kluwer Academic/Plenum.

Jessor, R. (1991). Risk behavior in adolescence: A psychological framework for understanding and action. *Journal of Adolescent Health,* 12, 597–605.

Johnson, J. L., & Wiechelt, S. A. (2004). Introduction to the special issue on resilience. *Substance Use and Misuse,* 39(5), 657–70.

Julianelle, P. F., & Foscarinis, M. (2003). Responding to the school mobility of children and youth experiencing homelessness: The McKinney–Vento Act and beyond. *Journal of Negro Education,* 72, 39–54.

Kaplan, H. B. (2005). Understanding the concept of resilience. In I. Goldstein & R. B. Brooks (Eds.), *Handbook of resilience in children* (pp. 39–47). New York: Kluwer Academic/Plenum.

Karabanow, J. (2008). Getting off the street: Exploring the processes of young people's street exits. *American Behavioral Scientist,* 51(6), 772–88.

Kazdin, A. (1993). Treatment of conduct disorder: Progress and directions in psychotherapy research. *Developmental Psychopathology,* 5, 277–310.

Kidd, S. A. (2004). "The walls were closing in, and we were trapped": A qualitative analysis of street youth suicide. *Youth and Society,* 36(1), 30–55.

Kipke, M. D., Palmer, R. F., LaFrance, S., & O'Conner, S. (1997a). Homeless youths' description of their parents' child-rearing practices. *Youth and Society,* 28(4), 415–31.

Kipke, M. D., Simon, T. R., Montgomery, S. B., Unger, J. B., & Iversen, E. F. (1997b). Homeless youth and their exposure to and involvement in violence while living on the streets. *Journal of Adolescent Health,* 20(5), 360–67.

Klopfenstein, K. (2004). Advanced Placement: Do minorities have equal opportunities? *Economics of Education Review*, 23(1), 115–31.

Kotlowitz, A. (1991). *There are no children here: The story of two boys growing up in the other America*. New York: Anchor Books.

Kozol, J. (1995). *Amazing grace: The lives of children and the conscience of a nation*. New York: HarperCollins.

—— (2005). *The shame of the nation: The restoration of apartheid schooling in America*. New York: Crown Publishing.

Kurtz, P. D., Jarvis, S. V., & Kurtz, G. L. (1991). Problems of homeless youths: Empirical findings and human services issues. *Social Work*, 36(4), 309–14.

LeBlanc, A. N. (2003). *Random family: Love, drugs, trouble, and coming of age in the Bronx*. New York: Scribner.

Liebow, E. (1993). *Tell them who I am: The lives of homeless women*. New York: Penguin Books.

Lifson, A. R., & Halcon, L. L. (2001). Substance abuse and high-risk needle-related behaviors among homeless youth in Minneapolis: Implications for prevention. *Journal of Urban Health*, 78(4), 690–98.

Lipsky, M. (1980). *Street-level bureaucracy: Dilemmas of the individual in public services*. New York: Russell Sage Foundation.

Los Angeles Coalition to End Hunger and Homelessness (2005). *Hunger and homelessness in Los Angeles 2006 fact sheet*. Retrieved on March 25, 2006, from www.lacehh.org.

Luthar, S., & Cicchetti, D. (2000). The construct of resilience: Implications for interventions and social policies. *Development and Psychopathology*, 12, 857–85.

Luthar, S. S., & Zelazo, L. B. (2003). Research on resilience. An integrative review. In S. S. Luthar (Ed.), *Resilience and vulnerability: Adaptation in the context of childhood adversities* (pp. 510–49). New York: Cambridge University Press.

McDonough, P., & Calderone, S. (2006) The meaning of money: Perceptual differences between college counselors and low-income families about college costs and financial aid. *American Behavioral Scientist*, 49(12), 1703–18.

MacKellar, D. A., Valleroy, L. A., Hoffmann, J. P., Glebatis, D., LaLota, M., McFarland, W., et al. (2000). Gender differences in sexual behaviors and factors associated with nonuse of condoms among homeless and runaway youths. *AIDS Education and Prevention*, 12(6), 477–91.

MacLeod, J. (1987, 1995). *Ain't no makin' it: Aspirations and attainment in a low-income neighborhood*. Boulder, CO: Westview Press.

McMillan, J. H., & Reed, D. F. (1994). At-risk students and resiliency: Factors contributing to academic success. *The Clearing House*, 67(3), 137–40.

McNeal, R. (1995). Extracurricular activities and high school dropouts. *Sociology of Education*, 68, 62–81.

Margolin, G., & Gordis, E. B. (2000). The effects of family and community violence on children. *Annual Review of Psychology*, 51, 445–79.

Masten, A. S. (1994). Resilience in individual development: Successful adaptation despite risk and adversity. In M. C. Wang & E. W. Gordon (Eds.), *Educational resilience in inner-city America: Challenges and perspectives* (pp. 3–25). Hillsdale, NJ: Erlbaum.

Masten, A. S., & Coatsworth, D. (1998). The development of competence in favorable and unfavorable environments: Lessons from research on successful children. *American Psychologist*, 53, 205–20.

Masten, A. S., Garmezy, N., Tellegen, A., Pellegrini, D. S., Larkin, K., & Larsen, A. (1988). Competence and stress in school children: The moderating effects of individual and family qualities. *Journal of Child Psychological Psychiatry*, 29, 745–64.

Masten, A. S., Miliotis, D., Graham-Bermann, S. A., Ramirez, M., & Neeman, J. (1993). Children in homeless families: Risks to mental health and development. *Journal of Consulting and Clinical Psychology*, 61(2), 335–43.

Masten, A. S., & Powell, J. L. (2003). A resilience framework for research, policy, and practice. In S. S. Luthar (Ed.), *Resilience and vulnerability: Adaptation in the context of childhood adversities* (pp. 1–21). New York: Cambridge University Press.

Masten, A. S., Sesma, A., Si-Asar, R., Lawrence, C., Miliotis, D., & Dionne, J. A. (1997). Educational risks for children experiencing homelessness. *Journal of School Psychology*, 35 (1), 27–46.

Mawhinney-Rhoads, L., & Stahler, G. (2006). Educational policy and reform for homeless students: An overview. *Education and Urban Society*, 38, 288–306.

Middlemiss, W. (2005). Prevention and intervention: Using resiliency-based multi-setting approaches and a process-orientation. *Child and Adolescent Social Work Journal*, 22(1), 85–103.

Murphy, L. B., & Moriarty, A. E. (1976). *Vulnerability, coping and growth: From infancy to adolescence.* New Haven, CT: Yale University Press.

National Alliance to End Homelessness (2006). *Promising strategies to end family homelessness.* Washington, DC: Author.

—— (2007). *Families reap substantial benefits under the Community Partnership to End Homelessness Act of 2007.* Washington, DC: Author.

National Center for Homeless Education (2007). *Education for homeless children and youth program: Analysis of 2005–2006 federal data collection and three-year comparison.* Greensboro, NC: Author.

O'Toole, T. P., Conde-Martel, A., Gibbon, J. L., Hanusa, B. H., Freyder, P. J., & Fine, M. J. (2007). Where do people go when they first become homeless? A survey of homeless adults in the USA. *Health and Social Care in the Community*, 15(5), 446–53.

Patton, M. Q. (2002). *Qualitative research and evaluation methods, third edition.* Thousand Oaks, CA: Sage.

Perna, L. W. (2006). Studying college choice: A proposed conceptual model. In J. C. Smart (Ed.), *Higher education: Handbook of theory and research, Vol. XXI.* (pp. 99–157). The Netherlands: Springer.

Perna, L. W., & Swail, S. W. (2001). Pre-college outreach and early intervention: An approach to achieving equal educational opportunity. *Thought and Action*, 17(1), 99–110.

Planty, M., Hussar, W., Snyder, T., Provasnik, S., Kena, G., Dinkes, R., *et al.* (2008). *The condition of education 2008 (NCES 2008–031).* Washington, DC: National Center for Education Statistics.

Quinton, D., Pickles, A., Maughan, B., & Rutter, M. (1993). Partners, peers, and pathways: Assortative pairing and continuities in conduct disorder. *Developmental Psychopathology*, 5, 763–83.

Rafferty, Y., & Rollins, N. (1989). *Learning in limbo: The educational deprivation of homeless children.* New York: Advocates for Children (ERIC Document Reproduction Service No. ED 312 363).

Randolph, K. A., Fraser, M. W., & Orthner, D. K. (2004). Educational resilience among youth at risk. *Substance Use and Misuse*, 39(5), 747–67.

Rausch, J. L., Lovett, C. R., & Walker, C. O. (2003). Indicators of resiliency among urban elementary school students at-risk. *The Qualitative Report*, 8(4), 570–590.

Reiss, D., Neiderhiser, J., Hetherington, E. M., & Plomin, R. (2000). *The relationship code: Deciphering genetic and social influences on adolescent development.* Cambridge, MA: Harvard University Press.

Rew, L., Fouladi, R. T., & Yockey, R. D. (2002). Sexual health practices of homeless youth. *Journal of Nursing Scholarship*, 34(2), 139–45.

Rew, L., Taylor-Seehafer, M., & Fitzgerald, M.L. (2001). Sexual abuse, alcohol and other drug use, and suicidal behaviors in homeless adolescents. *Issues in Comprehensive Pediatric Nursing*, 24(4), 225–40.

Rog, D. J., & Buckner, J. C. (2007). Homeless families and children. *Toward understanding homelessness: The 2007 National Symposium on Homelessness Research.* Washington, DC: US Department of Health and Human Services.

Rosenfeld, L. B., Lahad, M., & Cohen, A. (2001). Disaster, trauma, and children's resilience: A community response perspective. In J. M. Richman & M. W. Fraser (Eds.), *The context of youth violence: Resilience, risk and protection* (pp. 133–86). Westport, CT: Praeger.

Rutter, M. (1985). Resilience in the face of adversity: Protective factors and resistance to psychiatric disorder. *British Journal of Psychiatry*, 147, 598–611.

—— (1993). Resilience: Some conceptual considerations. *Journal of Adolescent Health*, 14, 626–31.

—— (2001). Psycholsocial adversity: Risk, resilience and recovery. In J. M. Richman & M. W. Fraser (Eds.), *The context of youth violence: Resilience, risk and protection* (pp. 13–42). Westport, CT: Praeger.

Sameroff, A., Gutman, L. M., & Peck, S. C. (2003). Adaptation among youth facing multiple risks: Prospective research findings. In S. S. Luthar (Ed.), *Resilience and vulnerability: Adaptation in the context of childhood adversities* (pp. 364–91). New York: Cambridge University Press.

Sandler, I. (2001). Quality and ecology of adversity as common mechanisms of risk and resilience. *American Journal of Community Psychology*, 29(1), 19–61.

Seidman, E., & Pederson, S., (2003). Holistic contextual perspectives on risk, protection, and competence among low-income urban adolescents. In S. S. Luthar (Ed.), *Resilience and vulnerability: Adaptation in the context of childhood adversities* (pp. 318–42). New York: Cambridge University Press.

Seifer, R., Sameroff, A. J., Baldwin, C. P., & Baldwin, A. (1992). Child and family factors that ameliorate risk between 4 and 13 years of age. *Journal of the American Academy of Child & Adolescent Psychiatry*, 31(5), 893–903.

Sheridan, S. M., Eagle, J. W., & Dowd, S. E. (2005). Families as contexts for children's adaptation. In I. Goldstein & R. B. Brooks (Eds.), *Handbook of resilience in children* (pp. 165–79). New York: Kluwer Academic/Plenum.

Shinn, M., Weitzman, B. C., Stojanovic, D., Knickman, J. R., Jimenez, L., Duchon, L., et al. (1998). Predictors of homelessness among families in New York City: From shelter request to housing stability. *American Journal of Public Health*, 88(11), 1651–57.

Shumow, L., Vandell, D. L., & Posner, J. (1999). Risk and resilience in the urban neighborhood: Predictors of academic performance among low-income elementary school children. *Merrill-Palmer Quarterly*, 45(2), 309–31.

Simons, R. L., & Whitbeck, L. B. (1991). Running away during adolescence as a precursor to adult homelessness. *Social Service Review*, 65(2), 224–44.

Smith, E. M., & Ferrari, J. R. (1997). *Diversity within the homeless population: Implications for intervention*. New York: Haworth Press.

Stack, C. (1974). *All our kin*. New York: Basic Books.

Stake, R. E. (2005). Qualitative case studies. In N. K. Denzin & Y. S. Lincoln (Eds.), *Sage handbook of qualitative research, third edition* (pp. 443–66). Thousand Oaks, CA: Sage.

Stanton-Salazar, R. (1997, 2001). *Manufacturing hope and despair: The school and kin support networks of US-Mexican youth*. New York: Teachers College Press.

Stronge, J. H. (1993). Emerging service delivery models for educating homeless children and youth: Implications for policy and practice. *Educational Policy*, 7(4), 447–65.

Suskind, R. (1999). *A hope in the unseen: An American odyssey from the inner city to the Ivy League*. New York: Broadway Books.

Tepper, P. (2004). *Homelessness in Los Angeles: A summary of recent research*. Institute for the Study of Homelessness & Poverty. Retrieved on October 3, 2004, from: www.weingart.org/institute.

Thompson, S. J., Maguin, E., & Pollio, D. E. (2003). National and regional differences among runaway youth using federally funded crisis services. *Journal of Social Service Research*, 30(1), 1–17.

Thompson, S. J., Safyer, A. W., & Pollio, D. E. (2001). Differences and predictors of family reunification among subgroups of runaway youths using shelter services. *Social Work Research*, 25(3), 163–72.

Thompson, S. J., Zittel-Palamara, K. M., & Maccio, E. M. (2004). Runaway youth utilizing crisis shelter services: Predictors of presenting problems. *Child and Youth Care Forum*, 33(6), 387–404.

Tierney, W. G., & Colyar, J. E. (Eds.) (2009). *Urban high school students and the challenge of access: Many routes, difficult paths (revised edition)*. New York: Peter Lang.

Tierney, W. G., Gupton, J. T., & Hallett, R. E. (2008). *Transition to adulthood for homeless adolescents*. Los Angeles, CA: Center for Higher Education Policy Analysis.

Tierney, W. G., & Hallett, R. E. (2010). Writing on the margins from the center: Homeless youth and cultural politics. *Cultural Studies Critical Methodologies*, 10(1), 19–27.

—— (forthcoming). Social capital and homeless youth: Influence of residential instability on college access. *Metropolitan Universities Journal*, 21.

Toro, P. A., & Warren, M. G. (1999). Homelessness in the United States: Policy considerations. *Journal of Community Psychology*, 27, 157–78.

Tyler, K. A., Hoyt, D. R., & Whitbeck, L. B. (2000). The effects of early sexual abuse on later sexual victimization among female homeless and runaway adolescents. *Journal of Interpersonal Violence*, 15(3), 235–50.

Unger, J. B., Kipke, M. D., Simon, T. R., Johnson, C. J., Montgomery, S. B., & Iverson, E. (1998). Stress, coping, and social support among homeless youth. *Journal of Adolescent Research*, 13(2), 134–57.

US Department of Health and Human Sciences (2006). *Child disposition and victimization rates, 2002–2006: Child maltreatment 2006*. Retrieved on December 26, 2008, from www.acf.hhs.gov/programs/cb/pubs/cm06/table3_2.htm.

Vance, J. E. (2001). Neurobiological mechanisms of psychosocial resiliency. In J. M. Richman & M. W. Fraser (Eds.), *The context of youth violence: Resilience, risk and protection* (pp. 43–82). Westport, CT: Praeger.

Walberg, H. J. (1984). Families as partners in educational productivity. *Phi Delta Kappan*, 65, 397–400.

Wang, M. C., Haertel, G. D., & Walberg, H. J. (Eds.) (1994). *Educational resilience in inner-city America: Challenges and prospects*. Hillsdale, NJ: Lawrence Erlbaum.

Waxman, H. C., Huang, S. L., & Padron, Y. N. (1997). Motivation and learning environment differences between resilient and nonresilient Latino middle school students. *Hispanic Journal of Behavioral Sciences*, 19, 137–55.

Werner, E. E., & Smith, R. S. (1982). *Vulnerable but invincible: A longitudinal study of resilient children and youth*. New York: McGraw Hill.

—— (1992). *Overcoming the odds: High risk children from birth to childhood*. Ithaca, NY: Cornell University Press.

Whitbeck, L. B., Hoyt, D. R., & Yoder, K. A. (1999). A risk-amplification model of victimization and depressive symptoms among runaway and homeless adolescents. *American Journal of Community Psychology*, 27(2), 273–96.

Whitbeck, L. B., & Simons, R. L. (1990). Life on the streets: The victimization of runaway and homeless adolescents. *Youth and Society*, 22(1), 108–25.

Willis, P. (1977). *Learning to labor: How working class kids get working class jobs*. New York: Columbia University Press.

Willis, T. A., Vaccaro, D., & McNamara, G. (1992). The role of life events, family support, and competence in adolescents' substance use: A test of vulnerability and protective factors. *American Journal of Communicative Psychology*, 20, 349–74.

Wirt, J., Choy, S., Rooney, P., Provasnik, S., Sen, A., & Tobin, R. (2004). *The condition of education 2004 (NCES 2004–077)*. Washington, DC: National Center for Education Statistics.

Witkin, A. L., Milburn, N. G., Rotheram-Borus, M. J., Batterham, P., May, S., & Brooks, R. (2005). Finding homeless youth: Patterns based on geographic area and number of homeless episodes. *Youth and Society*, 37(1), 62–84.

Wolch, J., Dear, M., Blasi, G., Flaming, D., Tepper, P., Koegel, P., *et al.* (2007). *Ending homelessness in Los Angeles: Inter-university consortium against homelessness.* Los Angeles: University of Southern California Center for Safer Cities.

Wright, B. R. E., Caspi, A., Moffitt, T. E., & Silva, P. A. (1998). Factors associated with doubled-up housing—a common precursor to homelessness. *Social Service Review*, 72(1), 92–111.

Wyman, P. A., Cowen, E. L., Work, W. C., & Parker, G. R. (1991). Developmental and family milieu correlates of resilience in urban children who have experienced major life stress. *American Journal of Community Psychology*, 19(3), 405–26.

Yates, G. L., MacKenzie, R., Pennbridge, J., & Cohen, E. (1988). A risk profile comparison of runaway and non-runaway youth. *American Journal of Public Health*, 78(7), 820–21.

Yates, T. M., Egeland, B., & Sroufe, L. A. (2003). Rethinking resilience: A developmental perspective. In S. S. Luthar (Ed.), *Resilience and vulnerability: Adaptation in the context of childhood adversities* (pp. 243–66). New York: Cambridge University Press.

Yin, R. K. (2003). *Case study research: Design and methods, third edition.* Thousand Oaks, CA: Sage Publications.

Yonezawa, S., Wells, A. S., & Serna, I. (2002). Choosing tracks: "Freedom of choice" in detracking schools. *American Educational Research Journal*, 39(1), 37–67.

Yossi, T. J. (2005). Whose culture has capital? A critical race theory discussion of community cultural wealth. *Race Ethnicity and Education*, 8(1), 69–91.

Zarate, E., & Pachon, H. R. (2006). *Perceptions of college financial aid among California Latino youth.* Los Angeles, CA: Tomas Rivera Policy Institute.

Zimmerman, M. A., & Arunkumar, R. (1994). Resiliency research: Implications for schools and policy. *Social Policy Report*, 8(4), 1–19.

Zimmerman, M. A., & Bingenheimer, J. B. (2002). Natural mentors and adolescent resiliency: A study with urban youth. *American Journal of Community Psychology*, 30(2), 221–43.

INDEX

Page references in *italics* denotes a table

Adelman, C. 26
adversity: and resilience 11–12
alcohol: and homeless youth 28; and study
  participants 116, 120

belief systems 13
Bender, K. 29
biological factors: and resilience 23
Birch, Herbert 20

case studies 31–2
Challenge Model *15*, 16–17, 19,
  105, 106
child abuse 25
Child and Family Services (CFS) 50
childrearing: and residential structure
  114–15, 117
Cicchetti, Dante 16
classroom instruction: influence of
  mobility on 113–14
Compensatory Model *15*, 17–18, 104–5,
  106
coping strategies 16, 19, 21, 25, 105
counselling 128
cultural customs: and doubled-up
  living 2

deficit perspective 11, 123
Department of Education (US) 2
depression: and homeless youth 10, 27–8

division of labor: in merged and separate
  households 7, 108, 114–15
doubled-up living/families 2; and
  cultural customs 2; developing
  programming and policies for 123–9;
  and economic necessity 3, 5; impact of
  economic downturn on 3–4, 32;
  influence of on study participants
  106–12; lack of research on 2; and
  lower-income families 3–4, 5; numbers
  experiencing 3, 4–5; supporting
  households 125–7; transitioning from
  shelter to 5
doubled-up youth: comparison with
  homeless youth 119–20; and
  education 4, 5, 6; and educational
  resilience 119–22, *120*; high rates of
  mobility 31, 32; inclusion in
  definition of homelessness 9, 124;
  non-identification with the term
  homeless 4, 124–5; reconsidering
  terms used to define 124–5; risk
  factors exposed to 31, 119; routines
  of life 31; social networks and
  support 10–11; *see also* study/study
  participants
drugs: and homeless youth 28; and study
  participants 53, 83, 105, 115, 116, 120,
  121, 132
Duneier, Mitchell 29

Echo Park (Los Angeles County) 33, *33*
economic downturn: impact of on doubled-up living 3–4, 32
educational experiences: and study participants 53–5, 66–7, 83–4, 96–8, 101
educational resilience 6, 7, 11–14; definition 13; and doubled-up youth 119–22, *120*
employment: and poverty 20
environmental risks: and educational outcomes of the homeless 10–11
Eyrich-Garg, Karen 10–11

family(ies): and homeless youth 28; influence on protective and risk factors 20, 23–4; supporting of by educational institutions 125–6; view of by study participants 107–8

gang violence: influence of on study participants 116
Gardner, Chris 15
Gayles, Jonathan 13
Gussow, Joan 20

Hammersley, Martyn 32
head of household 110–12
homeless liaison 124, 125, 126
homeless youth: barrier to college access 10; comparison with doubled-up youth 119–20; and deficit model 11; depression and suicidal ideation 10, 27–8; educational challenges 28; educational outcomes 10; educational rights and McKinney-Vento Homeless Assistance Act 9–10, 124; environmental and network factors influencing educational outcomes 10–11; and family 28; home environments 28; math proficiency and literacy 10; mental and physical health problems 27–8; protective factors associated with 29; and resilience 27–9; risk factors associated with 10, 27–8; sexual patterns of 28; and substance abuse 10, 28; transportation barriers 9
homelessness: definition 2; inclusion of doubled-up youth in definition of 9, 124; non-identification of with by doubled-up youth 4, 124–5; numbers experiencing 4

Invincibility Model 14–16, *15*, 104
Isaac (study participant) 30, 35, 38–9, 43–55, 103; background 8; basic demographic information *34*; day in the life of 45–50; educational experiences 53–5, 101; and educational resilience 121; epilogue 131–2; future aspirations 55; and models of resilience 104, 105; residential history 43–4, *44*, 50–2, 101; risk and protective factors 50–5; selection for study 35; social networks of 52–3; *see also* study/study participants

Juan (study participant) 1, 35, 37, 38, 56–68, 103, 128–9; background 8; basic demographic information *34*; day in the life of 57–63; educational experiences 66–7, 101; and educational resilience 121; epilogue 130–1; future aspirations 67–8; and models of resilience 104, 105; personality 56; residential history 56–7, *57*, 63–5; restricted access to residence of 36, 57; risk and protective factors 63–8; selection for study 35; social network of 65–6; *see also* study/study participants

Kidd, Sean 28
Kylee (study participant) 9–10, 35, 37, 38, 71–85, 103; background 8; basic demographic information *34*; day in the life of 72–9; educational experiences 83–4, 101; and educational resilience 121; epilogue 131; future aspirations 84–5; and models of resilience 104, 105; personality 71; residential history 71–2, *72*, 80–2; risk and protective factors 80–5; selection for study 35; social network 82–3; *see also* study/study participants

Liebow, Elliot 29
Lipsky, Michael 25
literacy: and homeless youth 10
Los Angeles County 32–3, *33*
Luthar, Suniya 16

McKinney-Vento Homeless Assistance Act 2, 4, 9, 124, 125, 126
Marco (study participant) 35, 36, 37, 38, 86–99, 103; background 8; basic demographic information *34*; day in the life of 87–93; educational experiences

96–8, 101; and educational resilience 121; epilogue 131; future aspirations 98–9; and models of resilience 104, 105; personality 86; residential history 86–7, *88*, 93–5; risk and protective factors 93–9; selection for study 35; social network 95–6; *see also* study/ study participants

mental health: and homeless youth 27–8; influence on risk and protective factors 21–3, *22*

mentoring 7, 14, 26, 27, 116

merged residences 7, 69–99, 108–10, *109*, 120, *120*, 125; approach to childrearing 114–15; and division of labor 7, 114–15; gender roles 118–19; head of household presence 110–11; as a protective factor 7, 69, 98, 108–12, 118–19, 120, 121–2; *see also* Kylee; Marco

mobility 28, 105; high rates of amongst doubled-up youth 31, 32; influence of on low rates of educational participation 10, 20, 28; influence on classroom instruction 113–14; influence of on social networks and relationships 10, 113; and perceived stability amongst study participants 113–14

motivation 13

neighborhood: influence of on risk and protective factors 24–6

networks *see* social networks

Parent Teacher Association 24

parents: influence on resilience 24; interactions with educational institutions 125–6

peer relationships 21, 27, 105, 107; impact of mobility on 113; as risk and protective factors 25–6

personal attributes 21–3

physical health: influence on risk and protective factors 21–2, *22*

policy and practice 123–9

postsecondary education: creating opportunities for 127–8

poverty: and employment 20; influence on low educational participation 20

protective factors 5, 6, 7, 11, 12, 13–14, 19–27; association with homeless youth 29; and Compensatory Model of resilience 17; definition and background

20–1; influence of family on 20, 23–4; influence of neighborhood on 24–6; influence of personal attributes on 21–3; influence of school on 26–7; influence of social networks on 22, 23–6; and merged households 7, 69, 98, 108–12, 118–19, 120, 121–2; neutralizing of risk factors by 17; and Protective Model of resilience *15*, 18, 105–6; and study participants 50–5, 63–8, 80–5, 93–9

Protective Model *15*, 18, 105–6, 106

quantitative studies 119

residential structure 103–22 *see also* merged residences; separate households

resilience 6, 9–29; and adversity 11–12; Challenge Model of *15*, 16–17, 19, 105, 106; Compensatory Model of *15*, 17–18, 104–5, 106; definition 11; educational 6, 7, 11–14, 119–22, *120*; and homeless youth 27–9; Invincibility Model of 14–16, *15*, 104; models of 14–18, 104–6; Protective Model of *15*, 18, 105–6; risk and protective factors 13–14, 19–27; and successful adaptation 11

Resiliency Theory 12–13, 14, 21, 112, 119

Rew, Lynn 28

risk factors 5, 6, 7, 13–14, 19–27; associated with homeless youth 10, 27–8; and Challenge Model 16–17; and Compensatory Model 17; definitions and background 19–20; exposure of doubled-up youth to 31, 119; influence of family on 23–4; influence of neighborhood on 24–6; influence of personal attributes on 21–3, *22*; influence of school on 26–7; influence of social networks on 22, 23–6; neutralizing of by protective factors 17; and separate households 7, 41, 110, 117–18, 120–1, 122; and study participants 40–5, 63–8, 80–5, 93–9

school: influence of on risk and protective factors 26–7

separate households 41–68, 108–10, *109*, 120–1, *120*; approach to childrearing 114–15; and division of labor 114–15; and head of household presence 111;

as a risk factor 7, 41, 110, 117–18, 120–1, 122; *see also* Isaac; Juan
sexual patterns: and homeless youth 28
shame, experience of 6, 35, 113, 119, 124
social environments: defining of by study participants 107–12; influence of on educational perceptions 112–17
social network programs 126–7
social networks: and doubled-up youth 10–11; and homeless youth 10; impact of mobility on 10, 113; importance of outside the home 121–2, 127; influence on risk and protective factors 22, 23–6; and study participants 52–3, 65–6, 82–3, 95–6
strength-based approach 6, 11, 12
study/study participants 30–9; defining their social environments 107–12; division of labor 114–15; drug and alcohol use 53, 83, 105, 115, 116, 120, 121, 132; educational resilience experienced 121; epilogue 130–2; gathering experiences of 35–6; influence of factors outside the residence 115–17; influence of gang violence on 116; influence of living doubled-up 106–19; influence of social environments on educational perceptions 112–17; and mentoring relationships 116; merged households as

a protective factor 7, 69, 98, 108–12, 118–19, 120, 121–2; mobility and perceived stability 113–14; and models of resilience 104–6; non-identification with the term homeless 4, 124–5; presence of a head of household 110–12; reviewing supporting materials 37; role of trust 37–8; selecting 32–5, 33; semi-structured interviews conducted 36–7; separate households as a risk factor 7, 41, 110, 117–18, 120–1, 122; social network factors outside of the home 121–2; view of family 107–8; *see also* Isaac; Juan; Kylee; Marco
substance use: and homeless youth 28; and study participants 53, 83, 105, 115, 116, 120, 121, 132
suicidal ideation: and homeless youth 10, 28
surveys 35
survival sex: and homeless youth 28
Suskind, Ron 15

Thompson, S.J. 28
trust: role of in study 37–8
twins 16

violence, exposure to 10, 16, 25

Watts (Los Angeles County) 33, 33